The Quick & Easy Way to Effective Speaking

GOLDEN MINDS

Published by:
Golden Minds Publishing House
326-330, Vardhaman Chambers,
Cawasji Patel Road, Kala Ghoda,
Fort, Mumbai - 400 001
email: goldenminds99@gmail.com

ISBN: 978-93-86341-16-7

Printed in India

CONTENTS

PART I

BASIC PRINCIPLES OF EFFECTIVE SPEAKING

Chapter 1

ACQUIRING THE BASIC SKILLS

I started teaching classes in public speaking in 1912, the year the Titanic went down in the icy waters of the North Atlantic.

Over the years, at these classes, people are given the opportunity of sharing what they hope to gain from this training. Naturally, the phraseology varies; but the central desire, the basic want in the vast majority of cases, remains surprisingly the same: "When I am called upon to stand up and speak, I become so self-conscious, so frightened, that I can't think clearly, can't concentrate, can't remember what I intended to say. I want to gain self-confidence, poise, and the ability to think on my feet. I want to get my thoughts together in logical order, and I want to be able to talk clearly and convincingly before a business or social group."

Does this sound familiar? Have you experienced these same feelings of inadequacy? Would you give a small fortune to have the ability to speak convincingly and persuasively in public? The very fact that you have begun reading the pages of this book is proof of your interest in acquiring the ability to speak effectively.

I know what you are going to say, what you would say if you could talk to me: "But Mr. Carnegie, do you really think I could develop the confidence to get up and face a group of people and

I have spent nearly all my life helping people get rid of their fears and develop courage and confidence. I could fill many books with the stories of the miracles that have taken place in my classes. It is not, therefore, a question of my *thinking*. I *know* you can, if you practice the directions and suggestions that you will find in this book.

Is there the faintest shadow of a reason why you should not be able to think as well in a perpendicular position before an audience as you can sitting down? Is there any reason why you should play host to butterflies in your stomach and become a victim of the "trembles" when you get up to address an audience? Surely, you realize that this condition can be remedied, that training and practice will wear away your audience-fright and give you self-confidence.

This book will help you to achieve that goal. It is not an ordinary textbook. It is not filled with rules concerning the mechanics of speaking. It does not dwell on the physiological aspects of vocal production and articulation. It is the distillation of a lifetime spent in training adults in effective speaking. It starts with you as you are, and from that premise works naturally to the conclusion of what you want to be. All you have to do is co-operate—follow the suggestions in this book, apply them in every speaking situation, and persevere.

In order to get the most out of this book, and to get it with rapidity and dispatch, you will find these four guideposts useful:

FIRST

Take Heart from Others' Experience

There is no such animal, in or out of captivity, as a

born public speaker. In those periods of history when public speaking was a refined art that demanded close attention to the laws of rhetoric and the niceties of delivery, it was even more difficult to be born a public speaker. Now we think of public speaking as a kind of enlarged conversation. Gone forever is the old grandiloquent style and the stentorian voice. What we like to hear at our dinner meetings, in our church services, on our TV sets and radios, is straightforward speech, conceived in common sense and dedicated to the proposition that we like speakers to talk with, and not at, us.

Despite what many school texts would lead us to believe, public speaking is not a closed art, to be mastered only after years of perfecting the voice and struggling with the mysteries of rhetoric. I have spent almost all of my teaching career proving to people that it is *easy* to speak in public, provided they follow a few simple, but important, rules. When I started to teach at the 125th Street YMCA in New York City back in 1912, I didn't know this any more than my first students knew it. I taught those first classes pretty much the way I had been taught in my college years in Warrensburg, Missouri. But I soon discovered that I was on the wrong track; I was trying to teach adults in the business world as though they were college freshmen. I saw the futility of using Webster, Burke, Pitt, and O'Connell as examples to imitate. What the members of my classes wanted was enough courage to stand on their hind legs and make a clear, coherent report at their next business meeting. It wasn't long before I threw the textbooks out the window, got right up there on the podium and, with a few simple ideas, worked with those fellows until they could give their reports in a convincing manner. It worked, because they kept coming back for more.

I wish I could give you a chance to browse through the

files of testimonial letters in my home or in the offices of my representatives in various parts of the world. They come from industrial leaders whose names are frequently mentioned in the business section of *The New York Times* and *The Wall Street Journal,* from governors of states and members of parliaments, from college presidents, and from celebrities in the world of entertainment. There are thousands more from housewives, ministers, teachers, young men and women whose names are not well known yet, even in their own communities, executives and executive trainees, laborers, skilled and unskilled, union men, college students, and business women. All of these people felt a need for self-confidence and the ability to express themselves acceptably in public. They were so grateful for having achieved both that they took the time to write me letters of appreciation.

Of the thousands of people I have taught, one example comes to mind as I write because of the dramatic impact it had on me at the time. Some years ago, shortly after he joined my course, D. W. Ghent, a successful businessman in Philadelphia, invited me to lunch. He leaned across the table and said: "I have sidestepped every opportunity to speak to various gatherings, Mr. Carnegie, and there have been many.

But now I am chairman of a board of college trustees.

I must preside at their meetings. Do you think it will be possible for me to learn to speak at this late date in life?"

I assured him, on the basis of my experience with men in similar positions who had been members of my classes, that there was no doubt in my mind that he would succeed.

About three years later we lunched together again at the Manufacturers' Club. We ate in the same dining room and at the very same table we had occupied at our first meeting. Reminding him of our former conversation, I asked him whether my prediction had come true. He smiled, took a little red-backed notebook out of his pocket, and showed me a list of speaking engagements for the next several months. "The ability to make these talks," he confessed, "the pleasure I get in giving them, the additional service I can render in the community–these are among the most gratifying things in my life."

But that was not all. With a feeling of justifiable pride, Mr. Ghent then played his ace card. His church group had invited the prime minister of England to address a convocation in Philadelphia. And the Philadelphian selected to make the introduction of the distinguished statesman, on one of his rare trips to America, was none other than Mr. D. W Ghent.

This was the man who had leaned across that same table less than three years before and asked me whether I thought he would ever be able to talk in public!

I have seen thousands of similar miracles worked in my courses. I have seen men and women whose lives were transformed by this training, many of them receiving promotions far beyond their dreams or achieving positions of prominence in their business, profession, and community. Sometimes this has been done by means of a single talk delivered at the right moment. Let me tell you the story of Mario Lazo.

Years ago, I received a cable from Cuba that astonished me. It read: "Unless you cable me to the contrary, I am coming to New York to take training to make a speech." It was signed: "Mario Lazo." Who was he? I wondered! I had never heard of him before.

When Mr. Lazo arrived in New York, he said: "The Havana Country Club is going to celebrate the fiftieth birthday of the founder of the club; and I have been invited to present him with a silver cup and to make the principal talk of the evening. Although I am an attorney, I have never made a public talk in my life. I am terrified at the thought of speaking. If I fail, it will be deeply embarrassing to my wife and myself socially; and, in addition, it might lower my prestige with my clients. That is why I have come all the way from Cuba for your help. I can stay only three weeks."

During those three weeks, I had Mario Lazo going from one class to another speaking three or four times a night. Three weeks later, he addressed the distinguished gathering at the Havana Country Club. His address was so outstanding that *Time* Magazine reported it under the head of foreign news and described Mario Lazo as a "silver-tongued orator."

Sounds like a miracle, doesn't it? It is a miracle—a twentieth century miracle of conquering fear.

SECOND

Keep Sight of Your Goal

When Mr. Ghent spoke of the pleasure his newly acquired skill in public speaking gave him, he touched upon what I believe (more than any other one factor) contributed to his success. It's true he followed the directions and faithfully did the assignments. But I'm sure he did these things because he wanted to do them, and he wanted to do them because he saw himself as a successful speaker. He projected himself into the future and then worked toward bringing that projection into reality. That is exactly what you must do.

Concentrate your attention on what self-confidence and the ability to talk more effectively will mean to you. Think of what it may mean to you socially, of the friends it will bring, of your increased capacity to be of service in your civic, social, or church group, of the influence you will be able to exert in your business. In short, it will prepare you for leadership.

In an article entitled "Speech and Leadership in

Business," S. C. Allyn, Chairman of the Board of the National Cash Register Company and Chairman of UNESCO, wrote in the *Quarterly Journal of Speech:* "In the history of our business, many a man has drawn attention to himself by a good job done on the platform. A good many years ago a young man, who was then in charge of a small branch in 'Kansas, gave a rather unusual talk, and is today our vice-president in charge of sales." I happen to know that this vice-president is now the president of the National Cash Register Company.

There is no predicting how far the ability to speak on your feet will take you. One of our graduates, Henry Blackstone, President of the Servo Corporation of America, says, "The ability to communicate effectively with others and win their co-operation is an asset we look for in men moving to the top."

Think of the satisfaction and pleasure that will be yours when you stand up and confidently share your thoughts and feelings with your audience. I have traveled around the world several times, but I know of few things that give greater delight than holding an audience by the power of the spoken word. You get a sense of strength, a feeling of power. "Two minutes before I begin," said one of my graduates, "I would rather be whipped than start; but two minutes before I finish, I would rather be shot than stop."

Begin now to picture yourself before an audience you might be called upon to address. See yourself stepping forward with confidence, listen to the hush fail upon the room as you begin, feel the attentive absorption of the audience as you drive home point after point, feel the warmth of the applause as you leave the platform, and hear the words of appreciation with which individual members of the audience greet you when the meeting is over. Believe me, there is a magic in it and a never-to-be forgotten thrill.

William James, Harvard's most distinguished professor of psychology, wrote six sentences that could have a profound effect on your life, six sentences that are the open sesame to Ali Baba's treasure cave of courage: "In almost any subject, your passion for the subject will save you. If you care enough for a result, you will most certainly attain it. If you wish to be good, you will be good. If you wish to be rich, you will be rich. If you wish to be learned, you will be learned. Only then you must really wish these things and wish them with exclusiveness and not wish one hundred other incompatible things just as strongly."

Learning to speak effectively to groups brings other benefits than merely the ability to make formal public speeches. As a matter of fact, if you never give a formal public speech in your life, the benefits to be derived from this training are manifold. For one thing, public speaking training is the royal road to self-confidence. Once you realize that you can stand up and talk intelligently to a group of people, it is logical to assume that you can talk to individuals with greater confidence and assurance. Many men and women have taken my course in Effective Speaking primarily because they were shy and self-conscious in social groups. When they found they were capable of speaking on their feet to their fellow class members without having the roof fall in, they became aware of the ridiculousness of self-consciousness. They began to impress others, their families, friends, business associates, customers, and clients, with their newly found poise. Many of our graduates, like Mr. Goodrich, were impelled to take the course by the remarkable change in the personalities of those around them.

This type of training also affects the personality in ways that are not immediately apparent. Not long ago I asked Dr. David Allman, the Atlantic City surgeon and former president of the American Medical Association, what in his opinion were the benefits of public speaking training in terms of mental and physical health. He smiled and said he could best answer that question by writing a prescription that "no drugstore can fill. It must be filled by the individual; if he thinks he can't, he is wrong."

I have the prescription on my desk. Every time I read it, I am impressed. Here it is, just as Dr. Allman jotted it down:

Try your best to develop an ability to let others look into your head and heart. Learn to make your thoughts, your ideas, clear to others, individually, in groups, in public. You will find, as you improve in your effort to do this, that you—your real self—are making an impression, an impact, on people such as you never made before.

You can reap a double benefit from this prescription. Your self-confidence strengthens as you learn to speak to others, and your whole personality grows warmer and better. This means that you are better off emotionally, and if you are better off emotionally, you are better off physically. Public speaking in our modern world is for everybody, men and women, young and elderly. I do not know personally about its advantages to one in business or industry. I only hear that they are great. But I do know its advantages in health. Speak when you can, to a few or to many; you will do it better and better, as I have found out, myself; and you will feel a buoyancy of spirit, a sense of being a whole, rounded person, such as you never felt before.

It is a wonderful sense to have, and no pill ever made can give it to you.

The second guidepost, then, is to picture yourself as successfully doing what now you fear to do, and to concentrate on the benefits you will receive through your ability to talk acceptably before groups. Remember the words of William James: "If you care enough for a result, you will most certainly attain it."

THIRD

Predetermine Your Mind to Success

I was asked once, on a radio program, to tell in three sentences the most important lesson I have ever learned. This is what I said: "The biggest lesson I have ever learned is the stupendous importance of what we think. If I knew what you think, I would know what you are, for your thoughts make you what you are. By changing our thoughts, we can change our lives."

You have set your sights on the goal of increased confidence and more effective communication. From now on, you must think positively, not negatively, about your chances to succeed in this endeavor. You must develop a buoyant optimism about the outcome of your efforts to speak before groups. You must set the seal of determination upon every word and action that you devote toward the development of this ability.

Here is a story that is dramatic proof of the need for resolute determination on the part of anyone who wants to meet the challenge of more expressive speaking. The man I am writing about has come up the management ladder so far that he has become a big business legend. But the first time he stood up to speak in college, words failed him. He couldn't get beyond the middle of the five-minute talk his teacher had assigned. His face went white, and he hurried off the platform in tears.

The man who had that experience as a young student didn't let that failure frustrate him. He determined to become a good speaker and didn't stop in that determination until he became a world-respected economic consultant to the government. His name is Clarence B. Randall. In one of his thoughtful books, *Freedom's Faith,* he has this to say about public speaking: "I have service stripes all the way up one sleeve and all the way down the other from appearances before luncheons and dinners of manufacturers' associations, Chambers of Commerce, Rotary Clubs, fund-raising campaigns, alumni organizations, and all the rest. I talked myself into World `War I by a patriotic address in Escanaba, Michigan; I have barnstormed for charity with Mickey Rooney, and for education with President James Bryant Conant of Harvard and Chancellor Robert M. Hutchins of the University of Chicago; and I have even made an after-dinner speech in very bad French.

"I think I know something about what an audience will listen to, and how they want it said. *And there is nothing whatever about it that a man worthy to bear important business responsibility cannot learn if he will."*

I agree with Mr. Randall. The will to succeed must be a vital part of the process of becoming an effective speaker. If I could look into your mind and ascertain the strength of your desire and the light and shadow of your thought I could foretell, almost with certainty, the swiftness of your progress toward your goal of improved communicative skills.

In one of my classes in the Middle West, a man stood up the first night and unabashedly said that as a builder of homes he wouldn't be content until he became a spokesman for the American Home Builders' Association. He wanted nothing more than to go up and down this country and tell everybody he met the problems and achievements of his industry. Joe Haverstick meant what he said. He was the kind of class member that delights an instructor: he was in dead earnest. He wanted to be able to talk, not on local issues only, but on national ones, and there was no half-heartedness about his desires. He prepared his talks thoroughly, practiced them carefully, and never missed a single session, though it was the busy season of the year for men in his business. He did precisely what such a class member always does—he progressed at a rate that surprised him. In two months he had become one of the outstanding members of the class. He was voted its president

The instructor handling that class was in Norfolk, Virginia, about a year later, and this is what he wrote: "I had forgotten all about Joe Haversack back in Ohio when, one morning while I was having breakfast, opened the *Virginia Pilot*. There was a picture of Joe and a write-up about him. The night before, he had addressed a large meeting of area builders, and I saw that Joe was not just a spokesman for the National Home Builders' Association; he was its president."

So, to succeed in this work, you need the qualities that are essential in any worthwhile endeavor: desire amounting to enthusiasm, persistence to wear away mountains, and the self-assurance to believe you will succeed.

When Julius Caesar sailed over the channel from Gaul and landed with his legions in what is now England, what did he do to insure the success of his army? A very clever thing: he halted his soldiers on the chalk cliffs of Dover; and, looking down over the waves two hundred feet below, they saw red tongues of fire consume every ship in which they had crossed. In the enemy's country, with the last link with the Continent gone, the last means of retreat burned, there was but one thing left for them to do: to advance, to conquer. That is precisely what they did.

Such was the spirit of the immortal Caesar. Why not make it yours, too, as you set out to conquer your fear of audiences? Throw every shred of negative thought into the consuming fires and slam doors of steel upon every escape into the irresolute past.

FOURTH

Seize Every Opportunity to Practice

The course I gave in the 125th Street YMCA before

World War I has been changed almost beyond recognition. Every year new ideas have been woven into the sessions and old ones cast away. But one feature of the course remains unchanged. Every member of every class must get up once, and in the majority of cases, twice, and give a talk before his fellow members. Why? Because no one can learn to speak in public without speaking in public any more than a person can learn to swim without getting in the water. You could read every volume ever written about public speaking—including this one—and still not be able to speak. This book is a thorough guide. But you must put its suggestions into practice.

When George Bernard Shaw was asked how he learned to speak so compellingly in public, he replied: "I did it the same way I learned to skate—by doggedly making a fool of myself until I got used to it." As a youth, Shaw was one of the most timid persons in London. He often walked up and down the Embankment for twenty minutes or more before venturing to knock at a door. "Few men," he confessed, "have suffered more from simple cowardice or have been more horribly ashamed of it."

Finally, he hit upon the best and quickest and surest method ever yet devised to conquer timidity, cowardice, and fear. He determined to make his weak point his strongest asset. He joined a debating society. He attended every meeting in London where there was to be a public discussion, and he always arose and took part in the debate. By throwing his heart into the cause of socialism, and by going out and speaking for that cause, George Bernard Shaw transformed himself into one of the most confident and brilliant speakers of the first half of the twentieth century.

Opportunities to speak are on all sides. Join organizations and volunteer for offices that will require you to speak. Stand up and assert yourself at public meetings, if only to second a motion. Don't take a back seat at departmental meetings. Speak up! Teach a Sunday School class. Become a Scout leader. Join any group where you will have an opportunity to participate actively in the meetings. You have but to look around you to see that there is scarcely a single business, community, political, professional, or even neighborhood activity that does not challenge you to step forward and speak up. You will never know what progress you can make unless you speak, and speak, and speak again.

"I know all about that," a young business executive once said to me, "but I hesitate to face the ordeal of learning."

"Ordeal!" I replied. "Put that thought out of your mind. You've never thought of learning in the right—the conquering—spirit."

"What spirit is that?" he asked.

"The spirit of adventure," I told him, and I talked to him a little about a path to success, through public speaking, and the warming up, the unfolding, of one's personality.

"I'll give it a try," he finally said. "I'll head into this adventure."

As you read on in this book, and as you put its principles into practice, you, too, will be heading into adventure. You will find it is an adventure in which your power of self-direction and your vision will sustain you. You will find it is an adventure that can change you, inside and out.

Don't wait for a huge platform before you give of your best performance.

—Bernard Kelvin Clive

Act enthusiastic and you will be enthusiastic.

—Dale Carnegie

Chapter 2

DEVELOP CONFIDENCE

"Five years ago, Mr. Carnegie, I came to the hotel where you were conducting one of your demonstrations. I walked up to the door of the meeting room and then stopped. I knew if I entered that room and joined a class, sooner or later I'd have to make a speech. My hand froze on the doorknob. I couldn't go in. I turned my back and walked out of the hotel.

"If I had only known then how you make it easy to conquer fear, the paralyzing fear of an audience, I wouldn't have lost these past five years."

The man who spoke these revealing words wasn't talking across a table or a desk. He was directing his remarks to an audience of some two hundred people. It was the graduation session of one of my courses in New York City. As he gave his talk, I was particularly impressed by his poise and self-assurance. Here was a man, I thought, whose executive skills will be tremendously increased by his newly acquired expressiveness and confidence. As his instructor, I was delighted to see that he had dealt a death blow to fear, and I couldn't help thinking how much more successful, and what is more, how much happier this man would have been if his victory over fear had come five or ten years before.

Emerson said, "Fear defeats more people than any other one thing in the world." Oh, how I have been made aware of the bitter truth of that statement. And how grateful I am that during my life I have been able to rescue people from fear. When I started to teach my course in 1912, little did I realize that this training would prove to be one of the best methods ever yet devised to help people eliminate their fears and feelings of inferiority. I found that learning to speak in public is nature's own method of overcoming self-consciousness and building up courage and self-confidence. Why? Because speaking in public makes us come to grips with our fears.

In years of training men and women to speak in public, I have picked up some ideas to help you quickly overcome stage fright and develop confidence in a few short weeks of practice.

FIRST

Get the Facts About Fear of Speaking in Public

You are not unique in your fear of speaking in public. Surveys in colleges indicate that eighty to ninety per cent of all students enrolled in speech classes suffer from stage fright at the beginning of the course. I am inclined to believe that the figure is higher among adults at the start of my course, almost one hundred per cent.

A certain amount of stage fright is useful! It is nature's way of preparing us to meet unusual challenges in our environment. So, when you notice your pulse beating faster and your respiration speeding up, don't become alarmed. Your body, ever alert to external stimuli, is getting ready to go into action. If these physiological preparations are held within limits, you will be capable of thinking faster, talking more fluently, and generally speaking with greater intensity than under normal circumstances.

Many professional speakers have assured me that they never completely lose all stage fright. It is almost always present just before they speak, and it may persist through the first few sentences of their talk. This is the price these men and women pay for being like race horses and not like draft horses. Speakers who say they are "cool as a cucumber" at all times are usually as thick-skinned as a cucumber and about as inspiring as a cucumber.

The chief cause of your fear of public speaking is simply that you are unaccustomed to speak in public. For most people, public speaking is an unknown quantity, and consequently one fraught with anxiety and fear factors. For the beginner, it is a complex series of strange situations, more involved than, say, learning to play tennis or drive a car. To make this fearful situation simple and easy: practice, practice, practice. You will find, as thousands upon thousands have, that public speaking can be made a joy instead of an agony merely by getting a record of successful speaking experiences behind you.

The story of how Albert Edward Wiggam, the prominent lecturer and popular psychologist, overcame his fear, has been an inspiration to me ever since I first read it. He tells how terror-struck he was at the thought of standing up in high school and delivering a five-minute declamation.

"As the day approached," he writes, "I became positively ill Whenever the dreadful thought occurred to me, my whole head would flush with blood and my cheeks would burn so painfully that I would go out behind the school building and press them against the cold brick wall to try to reduce their surging blushes. It was the same way with me in college.

"On one occasion, I carefully memorized a declamation beginning, 'Adam and Jefferson are no more.' When I faced the audience, my head was swimming so I scarcely knew where I was. I managed to gasp out the opening sentence, stating that 'Adams and Jefferson have passed away.' I couldn't say another word, so I bowed...and walked solemnly back to my seat amid great applause. The president got up and said, 'Well, Edward, we are shocked to hear the sad news, but we will do our best to bear up under the circumstances.' During the uproarious laughter that followed, death would surely have been a welcome relief. I was ill for days afterward.

"Certainly the last thing on earth I ever expected to become was a public speaker."

A year after he left college, Albert Wiggam was in Denver. The political campaign of 1896 was raging over the issue of Free Silver. One day he read a pamphlet explaining the proposals of the Free Silverites; he became so incensed over what he considered the errors and hollow promises of Bryan and his followers, that he pawned his watch for enough money to get back to his native Indiana. Once there, he offered his services to speak on the subject of sound money. Many of his old school friends were in the audience. "As I began," he writes, "the picture of my Adams and Jefferson speech in college swept over me. I choked and stammered and all seemed to be lost. But, as Chauncey Depew often said, both the audience and I managed somehow to live through the introduction; and encouraged by even this tiny success, I went on talking for what I thought was about fifteen minutes. To my amazement, I discovered I had been talking an hour and a half!

"As a result, within the next few years, I was the most surprised person in the world to find myself making my living as a professional public speaker.

"I knew at first hand what William James meant by the habit of success."

Yes, Albert Edward Wiggam learned that one of the

surest ways of overcoming the devastating fear of speaking before groups is to get a record of successful experiences behind you.

You should expect a certain amount of fear as a natural adjunct of your desire to speak in public, and you should learn to depend on a limited amount of stage fright to help make you give a better talk.

If stage fright gets out of hand and seriously curtails your effectiveness by causing mental blocks, lack of fluency, uncontrollable tics, and excessive muscular spasm, you should not despair. These symptoms are not unusual in beginners. If you make the effort, you will find the degree of stage fright soon reduced to the point where it will prove a help and not a hindrance.

SECOND

Prepare in the Proper Way

The principal speaker at a New York Rotary Club luncheon several years ago was a prominent government official. We were looking forward to hearing him describe the activities of his department.

It was obvious almost at once that he had not planned his speech. At first he tried to talk impromptu. Failing in that attempt, he pulled out of his pocket sheaf of notes which evidently had no more order than a flatcar full of scrap iron. He fumbled awhile with these, all the time becoming more embarrassed and inept in his delivery. Minute by minute he became more helpless, more bewildered. But he kept on floundering, apologizing, trying to make some semblance of sense out of his notes and raising a glass of water with a trembling hand to his parched lips. He was a sad picture of a man completely overcome by fright, due to almost total lack of preparation. He finally sat down, one of the most humiliated speakers I have ever seen. He made his talk as

Rousseau says a love letter should be written: he began without knowing what he was going to say, and finished without knowing what he had said.

Since 1912, it has been my professional duty to evaluate over five thousand talks a year. From that experience, one great lesson stands out like Mount Everest, towering above all the others: *only the prepared speaker deserves to be confident*. How can anyone ever hope to storm the fortress of fear if he goes into battle with defective weapons, or with no ammunition at all? "I believe," said Lincoln, "that I shall never be old enough to speak without embarrassment when I have nothing to say."

If you want to develop confidence, why not do the one thing that will give you security as a speaker? "Perfect love," wrote the Apostle John, "casteth out fear." So does perfect preparation. Daniel Webster said he would as soon think of appearing before an audience half-clothed as half-prepared.

Never memorize word for word: By "perfect preparation" do I mean that you should memorize your talk? To this question I give back a thunderous NO. In their attempts to protect their egos from the dangers of drawing a mental blank before an audience, many speakers fall headlong into the trap of memorization. Once a victim of this type of mental dope addiction, the speaker is hopelessly bound to a time-consuming method of preparation that destroys effectiveness on the platform.

When H. V. Kaltenborn, the dean of American news commentators, was a student at Harvard University, he took part in a speech contest. He selected a short story entitled "Gentlemen, the King." He memorized it word for word and rehearsed it hundreds of times. The day of the contest he announced the title, "Gentlemen, the King." Then his mind went blank. It not only went blank; it went black. He was terrified. In desperation he started telling the story in his own words. He was the most surprised boy in the hall when the judges gave him first prize. From that day to this, H. V. Kaltenborn has never read nor memorized a speech. That has been the secret of success in his broadcasting career. He makes a few notes and talks naturally to his listeners without a script.

The man who writes out and memorizes his talks is wasting his time and energy, and courting disaster. All our lives we have been speaking spontaneously. We haven't been thinking of words. We have been thinking of ideas. If our ideas are clear, the words come as naturally and unconsciously as the air we breathe.

Even Winston Churchill had to learn that lesson the hard way. As a young man, Churchill wrote out and memorized his speeches. Then one day, while delivering a memorized talk before the British Parliament, he stopped dead in his mental tracks. His mind went blank. He was embarrassed, humiliated! He began his last sentence all over again. Again his mind went blank and his face scarlet He sat down. From that day to this, Winston Churchill has never attempted to deliver a memorized talk.

If we memorize our talk word for word, we will probably forget it when we face our listeners. Even if we do not forget our memorized talk, we will probably deliver it in a mechanical way. Why? Because it will not come from our hearts, but from our memories. When talking with people privately, we always think of something we want to say, and then we go ahead and say it without thinking of words. We have been doing that all our lives. Why attempt to change it now? If we do write out and memorize our talks, we may have the same experience that Vance Bushnell had.

Vance was a graduate of the Beaux Arts School in Paris, and later became vice-president of one of the largest insurance companies in the world—the Equitable Life

Assurance Society. Years ago, he was asked to address a conference of two thousand Equitable Life representatives from all over America at a meeting in White Sulphur Springs, West Virginia. At that time, he had been in the life insurance business for only two years, but he had been highly successful, so he was scheduled to make a twenty-minute talk.

Vance was delighted to do so. He felt it would give him prestige. But, unfortunately, he wrote out and memorized his talk. He rehearsed forty times in front of a mirror. He had everything down pat: every phrase, every gesture, every facial expression. It was flawless, he thought.

However, when he stood up to deliver his address, he was terrified. He said: "My part in this program is...." His mind went blank. In his confusion, he took two steps backward and tried to start all over again. Again, his mind went blank. Again he took two steps back and tried to start. He repeated this performance three times. The platform was four feet high; there was no railing at the back; and there was a space five feet wide between the back of the platform and the wall. So, the fourth time he stepped back, he toppled backwards off the platform and disappeared into space. The audience howled with laughter. One man fell off his chair and rolled in the aisle. Never before nor since in the history of the Equitable Life Assurance Society has anyone ever given such a comic performance. The astonishing part of the story is that the audience thought it was really an act. The old-timers of the Equitable Life are still talking about his performance.

But what about the speaker, Vance Bushnell? Vance Bushnell himself told me it was the most embarrassing occasion of his life. He felt so disgraced that he wrote out his resignation.

Vance Bushnell's superiors persuaded him to tear up his

resignation. They restored his self-confidence; and Vance Bushnell, in later years, became one of the most effective speakers in his organization. But he never memorized a talk again. Let us profit by his experience.

I have heard countless scores of men and women try to deliver memorized talks, but I don't remember even one speaker who wouldn't have been more alive, more effective, more human, if he had tossed his memorized talk into the waste basket. If he had done that, he might have forgotten some of his points. He might have rambled, but at least he would have been human.

Abe Lincoln once said: "I don't like to hear a cut-and-dried sermon. When I hear a man preach, I like to see him act as if he were fighting bees." Lincoln said he wanted to hear a speaker cut loose and get excited. No speaker ever acts as if he were fighting bees when he is trying to recall memorized words.

Assemble and Arrange Your Ideas Beforehand: What, then, is the proper method of preparing a talk? Simply this: search your background for significant experiences that have taught you something about life, and assemble *your* thoughts, *your* ideas, *your* convictions, that have welled up from these experiences. True preparation means brooding over your topics. As Dr. Charles Reynold Brown said some years ago in a memorable series of lectures at Yale University: "Brood over your topic until it becomes mellow and expansive... then put all these ideas down in writing, just a few words, enough to fix the idea...put them down on scraps of paper—you will find it easier to arrange and organize these loose bits when you come to set your material in order." This doesn't sound like such a difficult program, does it? It isn't. It just requires a little concentration and thinking to a purpose.

Rehearse Your Talk: Should you rehearse your talk after

you have it in some kind of order? By all means. Here is a sure-fire method that is easy and effective. Use the ideas you have selected for your talk in everyday conversation with your friends and business associates. Instead of going over the ball scores, just lean across the luncheon table and say something like this: "You know, Joe, I had an unusual experience one day. I'd like to tell you about it." Joe will probably be happy to listen to your story. Watch him for his reactions. Listen to his response. He may have an interesting idea that may be valuable. He won't know that you are rehearsing your talk, and it really doesn't matter. But he probably will say that he enjoyed the conversation.

Allan Nevins, the distinguished historian, gives similar advice to writers: "Catch a friend who is interested in the subject and talk out what you have learned at length. In this way you discover facts of interpretation that you might have missed, points of arguments that had been unrealized, and the form most suitable for the story you have to tell."

THIRD

Predetermine Your Mind to Success

In the first chapter, you remember, this sentence was used in reference to building the right attitude toward public speaking training in general. The same rule applies to the specific task now facing you, that of making each opportunity to speak a successful experience. There are three ways to accomplish this:

Lose Yourself in Your Subject: After you have selected your subject, arranged it according to plan, and rehearsed it by "talking it out" with your friends, your preparation is not ended. You must sell yourself on the importance of your subject You must have the attitude that has inspired all the truly great personages of history—a belief in your cause. How do you fan the fires of faith in your message? By exploring all phases of your subject, grasping its deeper meanings, and asking yourself how your talk will help the audience to be better people for having listened to you.

Keep Your Attention Off Negative Stimuli: For instance, thinking of yourself making errors of grammar or suddenly coming to an end of your talk somewhere in the middle of it is certainly a negative projection that could cancel confidence before you started. It is especially important to keep your attention off yourself just before your turn to speak. Concentrate on what the other speakers are saying, give them your wholehearted attention and you will not be able to work up excessive stage fright.

Give Yourself a Pep Talk: Unless he is consumed by some great cause to which he has dedicated his life, every speaker will experience moments of doubt about his subject matter. He will ask himself whether the topic is the right one for him, whether the audience will be interested in it. He will be sorely tempted to change his subject. At times like these, when negativism is most likely to tear down self-confidence completely, you should give yourself a pep talk. In clear, straightforward terms tell yourself that your talk is the right one for you, because it comes out of your experience, out of your thinking about life. Say to yourself that you are more qualified than any member of the audience to give this particular talk and, by George, you are going to do your best to put it across. Is this old-fashioned Coupe teaching? It may be, but modern experimental psychologists now agree that motivation based on autosuggestion is one of the strongest incentives to rapid learning, even when simulated. How much more powerful, then, will be the effect of a sincere pep talk based on the truth?

FOURTH

Act Confident

The most famous psychologist that America has

produced, Professor William James, wrote as follows:

"Action seems to follow feeling, but really action and feeling go together; and by regulating the action, which is under the more direct control of the will, we can indirectly regulate the feeling, which is not.

"Thus the sovereign voluntary path to cheerfulness, if our spontaneous cheerfulness be lost, is to sit up cheerfully and to act and speak as if cheerfulness were already there. If such conduct does not make you feel cheerful, nothing else on that occasion can.

"So, to feel brave, act as if we were brave, use all of our will to that end, and a courage-fit will very likely replace the fit of fear."

Apply Professor James' advice. To develop courage when you are facing an audience, act as if you already had it. Of course, unless you are prepared, all the acting in the world will avail but little. But granted that you know what you are going to talk about, step out briskly and take a deep breath. In fact, breathe deeply for thirty seconds before you ever face your audience. The increased supply of oxygen will buoy you up and give you courage. The great tenor, Jean de Reszke, used to say that when you had your breath so you "could sit on it", nervousness vanished.

Draw yourself up to your full height and look your audience straight in the eyes, and begin to talk as confidently as if every one of them owed you money. Imagine that they do. Imagine that they have assembled there to beg you for an extension of credit. The psychological effect on you will be beneficial.

If you doubt that this philosophy makes sense, take the word of an American who will always be a symbol of courage. Once he was the most timorous of men; by practicing self-assurance, he became one of the boldest; he was the trust-busting, audience-swaying, Big-Stick-wielding President of the United States, Theodore Roosevelt.

"Having been a rather sickly and awkward boy," he confesses in his autobiography, "I was, as a young man, at the first both nervous and distrustful of my powers. I had to train myself painfully and laboriously not merely as regards my body but as regards my soul and spirit."

Fortunately, he has disclosed how he achieved the transformation. "When a boy," he wrote, "I read a passage in one of Marryat's books which always impressed me. In this passage, the captain of some small British man-of-war is explaining to the hero how to acquire the quality of fearlessness. He says that at the outset almost every man is frightened when he goes into action, but that the course to follow is for the man to keep such a grip on himself that he can act just as if he were not frightened. After this is kept up long enough, it changes from pretense to reality, and the man does in very fact become fearless by sheer dint of practicing fearlessness when he does not feel it.

"This was the theory upon which I went. There were all kinds of things of which I was afraid at first, ranging from grizzly bears to 'mean' horses and gunfighters; but by acting as if I were not afraid I gradually ceased to be afraid. Most men can have the same experience if they choose."

Overcoming fear of public speaking has a tremendous transfer value to everything that we do. Those who answer this challenge find that they are better persons because of it. They find that their victory over fear of talking before groups has taken them out of themselves into a richer and fuller life.

A salesman wrote: "After a few times on my feet before the class, I felt that I could tackle anyone. One morning I walked up to the door of a particularly tough purchasing agent, and before he could say 'no,' I had my samples spread out on his desk, and he gave me one of the biggest orders I have ever received."

A housewife told one of our representatives: "I was afraid to invite the neighbors in for fear that I wouldn't be able to keep the conversation going. After taking a few sessions and getting up on my feet, I took the plunge and held my first party. It was a great success. I had no trouble stimulating the group along interesting lines of talk."

At a graduating class, a clerk said: "I was afraid of the customers, I gave them a feeling that I was apologetic. After speaking to the class a few times, I found that I was speaking up with more assurance and poise, I began to answer objections with authoritativeness. My sales went up forty-five per cent the first month after I started to speak to this class."

They discovered that it was easy to conquer other fears and anxieties and to be successful where before they may have failed. You, too, will be able to meet the problems and conflicts of life with a new sense of mastery. What has been a series of insoluble situations can become a bright challenge to increased pleasure in living.

> *To be yourself in a world that is constantly trying to make you something else is the greatest accomplishment.*
>
> *—Ralph Waldo Emerson*

Chapter 3

SPEAK EFFECTIVELY, THE QUICK AND EASY WAY

I seldom watch television in the daytime. But a friend recently asked me to listen to an afternoon show that was directed primarily to housewives. It enjoyed a very high rating, and my friend wanted me to listen because he thought the audience participation part of the show would interest me. It certainly did. I watched it several times, fascinated by the way the master of ceremonies succeeded in getting people in the audience to make talks in a way that caught and held my attention. These people were obviously not professional speakers. They had never been trained in the art of communication. Some of them used poor grammar and mispronounced words. But all of them were interesting. When they started to talk they seemed to lose all fear of being on camera and they held the attention of the audience.

Why was this? I know the answer because I have been employing the techniques used in this program for many years. These people, plain, ordinary men and women, were holding the attention of viewers all over the country; they were talking about themselves, about their most embarrassing moments, their most pleasant memory, or how they met their wives or husbands. They were not thinking of introduction, body, and conclusion. They were not concerned with their diction or their sentence structure. Yet they were getting the final seal of approval from the audience—complete attention in what they had to say. This is dramatic proof of what to me is the first of three cardinal rules for a quick and easy way to learn to speak in public:

FIRST

Speak About Something You Have Earned the Right to Talk About Through Experience or Study

The men and women whose live flesh-and-blood stories made that television program interesting were talking from their own personal experience. They were talking about something they knew. Consider what a dull program would have resulted if they had been asked to define communism or to describe the organizational structure of the United Nations. Yet that is precisely the mistake that countless speakers make at countless meetings and banquets. They decide they must talk about subjects of which they have little or no personal knowledge and to which they have devoted little or no attention. They pick a subject like Patriotism, or Democracy, or Justice, and then, after a few hours of frantic searching through a book of quotations or a speaker's handbook for all occasions, they hurriedly throw together some generalizations vaguely remembered from a political science course they once took in college, and proceed to give a talk distinguished for nothing other than its length. It never occurs to these speakers that the audience might be interested in factual material bringing these high-flown concepts down to earth.

At an area meeting of Dale Carnegie instructors in the Conrad Hilton Hotel in Chicago some years ago, a student speaker started like this: "Liberty, Equality, Fraternity. These are the mightiest ideas in the dictionary of mankind. Without liberty, life is not worth living. Imagine what existence would be like if your freedom of action would be restricted on all sides."

That is as far as he got, because he was wisely stopped by the instructor, who then asked him why he believed what he was saying. He was asked whether he had any proof or personal experience to back up what he had just told us. Then he gave us an amazing story.

He had been a French underground fighter. He told us of the indignities he and his family suffered under Nazi rule. He described in vivid language how he escaped from the secret police and how he finally made his way to America. He ended by saying: "When I walked down Michigan Avenue to this hotel today, I was free to come or go, as I wished. I passed a policeman and he took no notice of me. I walked into this hotel without having to present an identification card, and when this meeting is over I can go anywhere in Chicago I choose to go. Believe me, freedom is worth fighting for." He received a standing ovation from that audience.

TELL US WHAT LIFE HAS TAUGHT YOU

Speakers who talk about what life has taught them never fail to keep the attention of their listeners. I know from experience that speakers are not easily persuaded to accept this point of view—they avoid using personal experiences as too trivial and too restrictive. They would rather soar into the realms of general ideas and philosophical principles, where unfortunately the air is too rarefied for ordinary mortals to breathe. They give us editorials when we are hungry for the news. None of us is averse to listening to editorials, when they are given by a man who has earned the right to editorialize—an editor or publisher of a newspaper. The point, though, is this: Speak on what life has taught you and I will be your devoted listener. It was said of Emerson that he was always willing to listen to any man, no matter how humble his station, because he felt he could learn something from every man he met. I have listened to more adult talks, perhaps, than any other man west of the Iron Curtain, and I can truthfully say that I have never heard a boring talk when the speaker related what life had taught him, no matter how slight or trivial the lesson may have been.

To illustrate: Some years ago, one of our instructors conducted a course in public speaking for the senior officers of New York City banks. Naturally, the members of such a group, having many demands upon their time, frequently found it difficult to prepare adequately, or to do what they conceived of as preparing. All their lives they had been thinking their own individual thoughts, nurturing their own personal convictions, seeing things from their own distinctive angles, living their own original experiences. They had spent forty years storing up material for talks. But it was hard for some of them to realize that.

One Friday a certain gentleman connected with an uptown bank—for our purposes we shall designate him as Mr. Jackson—found four-thirty had arrived, and what was he to talk about? He walked out of his office, bought a copy of *Forbes' Magazine* at a newsstand, and in the subway coming down to the Federal Reserve Bank where the class met, he read an article entitled, "You Have Only Ten Years to Succeed." He read it, not because he was interested in the article especially, but because he had to speak on something to fill his quota of time.

An hour later, he stood up and attempted to talk convincingly and interestingly on the contents of this article.

What was the result, the inevitable result?

He had not digested, had not assimilated what he was trying to say. "Trying to say"—that expresses it precisely. He was *trying*. There was no real message in him seeking for an outlet; and his whole manner and tone revealed it unmistakably. How could he expect the audience to be any more impressed than he himself was? He kept referring to the article, saying the author said so and so. There was a surfeit of *Forbes' Magazine* in it, but regrettably little of Mr. Jackson.

After he finished his talk, the instructor said, "Mr. Jackson, we are not interested in this shadowy personality who wrote that article. He is not here. We can't see him. But we are interested in you and your ideas. Tell us what you think, personally, not what somebody else said. Put more of Mr. Jackson in this. Would you take this same subject next week? Read this article again, and ask yourself whether you agree with the author or not. If you do, illustrate the points of agreement with observations from your own experience. If you don't agree with him, tell us why. Let this article be the starting point from which to launch your own talk."

Mr. Jackson reread the article and concluded that he did not agree with the author at all. He searched his memory for examples to prove his points of disagreement. He developed and expanded his ideas with details from his own experience as a bank executive. He came back the next week and gave a talk that was full of his own convictions, based on his own background. Instead of a warmed-over magazine article, he gave us ore from his own mine, currency coined in his own mint. I leave it to you to decide which talk made a stronger impact on the class.

LOOK FOR TOPICS IN YOUR BACKGROUND

Once a group of our instructors were asked to write on a slip of paper what they considered was the biggest problem they had with beginning speakers. When the slips were tallied, it was found that "getting beginners to talk on the right topic" was the problem most frequently encountered in early sessions of my course.

What is the right topic? You can be sure you have the right topic for you if you have lived with it, made it your own through experience and reflection. How do you find topics? By dipping into your memory and searching your background for those significant aspects of your life that made a vivid impression on you. Several years ago, we made a survey of topics that held the attention of listeners in our classes. We found that the topics most approved by the audience were concerned with certain fairly defined areas of one's background:

Early Years and Upbringing. Topics that deal with the family, childhood memories, schooldays, invariably get attention, because most of us are interested in the way other people met and overcame obstacles in the environment in which they were reared.

Whenever possible, work into your talks illustrations and examples from your early years. The popularity of plays, movies, and stories that deal with the subject of meeting the challenges of the world in one's early years attests to the value of this area for subject matter of talks. But how can you be sure anyone will be interested in what happened to you when you were young? There's one test. If something stands out vividly in your memory after many years have gone by, that almost guarantees that it will be of interest to an audience.

Early Struggles to Get Ahead. This is an area rich in human interest. Here again the attention of a group can be held by recounting your first attempts to make your mark on the world. How did you get into a particular job or profession? What twist of circumstances accounted for your career? Tell us about your setbacks, your hopes, your triumphs when you were establishing yourself in the competitive world. A real-life picture of almost anyone's life—if told modestly—is almost surefire material.

Hobbies and Recreation. Topics in this area are based on personal choice and, as such, are subjects that command attention. You can't go wrong talking about something you do out of sheer enjoyment. Your natural enthusiasm for your particular hobby will help get this topic across to any audience.

Special Areas of Knowledge. Many years of working in the same field have made you an expert in your line of endeavor. You can be certain of respectful attention if you discuss aspects of your job or profession based on years of experience or study.

Unusual Experiences. Have you ever met a great man? Were you under fire during the war? Have you gone through a spiritual crisis in your life? These are experiences that make the best kind of speech material.

Beliefs and Convictions. Perhaps you have given a great deal of time and effort to thinking about your position on vital subjects confronting the world today. If you have devoted many hours to the study of issues of importance, you have earned the right to talk about them. But when you do, be certain that you give specific instances for your convictions. Audiences do not relish a talk filled with generalizations. Please don't consider the casual reading of a few newspaper articles sufficient preparation to talk on these topics. If you know little more about a subject than the people in your audience, it is best to avoid it. On the other hand, if you have devoted years of study to some subject, it is undoubtedly a topic that is made to order for you. By all means, use it

As was pointed out in Chapter Two, the preparation of a talk does not consist merely in getting some mechanical words down on paper, or in memorizing a series of phrases. It does not consist in lifting ideas secondhand from some hastily read book or newspaper article. But it does consist in digging deep into your mind and heart and bringing forth some of the essential convictions that life has stored there. Never doubt that the material is there. It is! Rich stores of it, waiting for you to discover it. Do not spurn such material as too personal, too slight for an audience to hear. I have been highly entertained and deeply moved by such talks, more entertained and more moved than I have been by many professional speakers.

Only by talking about something you have earned the right to talk about will you be able to fulfill the second requirement for learning to speak in public quickly and easily. Here it is:

SECOND

Be Sure You Are Excited About Your Subject

Not all topics that you and I have earned the right to talk about make us excited. For instance, as a do-it yourself devotee, I certainly am qualified to talk about washing dishes. But somehow or other I can't get excited about this topic. As a matter of fact, I would rather forget about it altogether. Yet I have heard housewives—household executives, that is—give superb talks about this same subject. They have somehow aroused within themselves such a fury of indignation about the eternal task of washing dishes, or they have developed such ingenious methods of getting around this disagreeable chore, that they have become really excited about it. As a consequence, they have been able to talk effectively about this subject of washing dishes. Here is a question that will help you determine the suitability of topics you feel qualified to discuss in public: if someone stood up and directly opposed your point of view, would you be impelled to speak with conviction and earnestness in defense of your position? If you would, you have the right subject for you.

Recently, I came across some notes I had written in 1926 after I had visited the Seventh Session of the League of Nations in Geneva, Switzerland. Here is a paragraph: "After three or four lifeless speakers read their manuscripts, Sir George Foster of Canada took the floor. With immense satisfaction I noted that he had no papers or notes of any kind. He gestured almost constantly. His heart was in what he was saying. He had something he very much wanted to get across. The fact that he was earnestly trying to convey to the audience certain convictions that he cherished in his own heart was as plain as Lake Geneva outside the windows. Principles I have been advocating in my teaching were beautifully illustrated in that talk."

I often recall that speech by Sir George. He was sincere; he was earnest. Only by choosing topics which are felt by the heart as well as thought out by the mind will this sincerity be made manifest. Bishop Fulton J. Sheen, one of America's most dynamic speakers, learned this lesson early in life.

"I was chosen for the debating team in college," he wrote in his book, *Life Is Worth Living,* "and the night before the Notre Dame debate, our professor of de bating called me to his office and scolded me.

" 'You are absolutely rotten. We have never had anybody in the history of this college who was a worse speaker than yourself.'

" 'Well,' I said, trying to justify myself, `if I am so rotten why did you pick-me for the team?'

" 'Because,' he answered, 'you can think; not because you can talk. Get over in that corner. Take a paragraph of your speech and go through it.' I repeated a paragraph over and over again for an hour, at the end of which he said, 'Do you see any mistake in that?' `No.' Again an hour and a half, two hours, two and a half hours, at the end of which I was exhausted. He said, 'Do you still not see what is wrong?'

"Being naturally quick, after two hours and a half, I caught on. I said, 'Yes, I am not sincere. I am not myself. I do not talk as if I meant it.' "

At this point, Bishop Sheen learned a lesson he always remembered: *he put himself into his talk.* He became excited about his subject matter. Only then the wise professor said, "Now, you are ready to speak!"

When a member of one of our classes says, "I don't get excited about anything, I lead a humdrum sort of life," our instructors are trained to ask him what he does in his spare time. One goes to the movies, another bowls, and another cultivates roses. One man told his instructor that he collected books of matches. As the instructor continued to question him about this unusual hobby, he gradually became animated. Soon he was using gestures as he described the cabinets in which he stored his collection. He told his instructor that he had match books from almost every country in the world. When he became excited about his favorite topic, the instructor stopped him. "Why don't you tell us about this subject? It sounds fascinating to me." He said that he didn't think anyone would be interested! Here was a man who had spent years in pursuit of a hobby that was almost a passion with him; yet he was negative about its value as a topic to speak about. This instructor assured this man that the only way to gauge the interest value of a subject was to ask yourself how interested you are in it. He talked that night with all the fervor of the true collector, and I heard later that he gained a certain amount of local recognition by going to various luncheon clubs and talking about match book collecting.

This illustration leads directly to the third guiding principle for those who want a quick and easy way to learn to speak in public.

THIRD

Be Eager to Share Your Talk with Your Listeners

There are three factors in every speaking situation: the speaker, the speech or the message, and the audience. The first two rules in this chapter dealt with the interrelationships of the speaker to a speech. Up to this point there is no speaking situation. Only when the speaker relates his talk to a living audience will the speaking situation come to life. The talk may be well prepared; it may concern a topic which the speaker is excited about; but for complete success, another factor must enter into his delivery of the talk. He must make his listeners feel that what he has to say is important to them. He must not only be excited about his topic, but he must be eager to transfer this excitement to his listeners. In every public speaker of note in the history of eloquence, there has been this unmistakable quality of salesmanship, evangelism, call it what you will. The effective speaker earnestly desires his listeners to feel what he feels, to agree with his point of view, to do what he thinks is right for them to do, and to enjoy and relive his experience with him. He is audience-centered and not self-centered. He knows that the success or failure of his talk is not for him to decide–it will be decided in the minds and hearts of his hearers.

I trained a number of men in the New York City Chapter of the American Institute of Banking to speak during a thrift campaign. One of the men in particular wasn't getting across to his audience. The first step in helping that man was to fire up his mind and heart withthink over this subject until he became enthusiastic about it. I asked him to remember that the Probate Court Records in New York show that more than 85 per cent of the people leave nothing at all at death; that only 3.3 per cent leave $10,000 or over. He was to keep constantly in mind that he was not asking people to do him a favor or something that they could not afford to do. He was to say to himself: "I am preparing these people to have meat and bread and clothes and comfort in their old age, and to leave their wives and children secure." He had to remember he was going out to perform a great social service. In short, he had to be a crusader.

He thought over these facts. He burned them into his mind. He aroused his own interest, stirred his own enthusiasm, and came to feel that he, indeed, had a mission. Then, when he went out to talk, there was a ring to his words that carried conviction. He sold his listeners on the benefits of thrift because he had an eager desire to help people. He was no longer just a speaker armed with facts; he was a missionary seeking converts to a worthwhile cause.

At one time in my teaching career I relied considerably on the textbook rules of public speaking. In doing this I was merely reflecting some of the bad habits that had been instilled into me by teachers who had not broken away from the stilted mechanics of elocution.

I shall never forget my first lesson in speaking. I was taught to let my arm hang loosely at my side, with the palm turned to the rear, fingers half-closed and thumb touching my leg. I was drilled to bring the arm up in a picturesque curve, to give the wrist a classical turn, and then to unfold the forefinger first, the second finger next, and the little finger last. When the whole aesthetic and ornamental movement had been executed, the arm was to retrace the course of the curve and rest again by the side of the leg. The whole performance was wooden and affected. There was nothing sensible or honest about it.

My instructor made no attempt to get me to put my own individuality into my speaking; no attempt to have me speak like a normal, living human being conversing in an energetic manner with my audience.

Contrast this mechanistic approach to speech training with the three primary rules I have been discussing in this chapter. They are the basis of my entire approach to training in effective speaking. You will come across them again and again in this book.

A speaker should approach his preparation not by what he wants to say, but by what he wants to learn.

—Todd Stocker

For better or worse, you must play your own instrument in the orchestra of life

—Dale Carnegie

PART II

TECHNIQUES OF EFFECTIVE SPEAKING

Chapter 4

INTRODUCING SPEAKERS, PRESENTING AND ACCEPTING AWARDS

When you are called upon to speak in public, you may introduce another speaker or make a longer talk to inform, entertain, convince, or persuade. Perhaps you are program chairman of a civic organization or a member of a women's club and you face the task of introducing the main speaker at your next meeting, or perhaps you are looking forward to the time when you will address the local PTA, your sales group, a union meeting, or a political organization. In Chapter Thirteen, I will give you hints on preparing the longer type of talk, and this chapter will help you to prepare a speech of introduction. I shall give you also some valuable hints on presenting and accepting awards.

John Mason Brown, the writer and lecturer, whose lively talks have won audiences everywhere in the country, was speaking one night with the man who was to introduce him to his audience.

"Stop worrying about what you are going to say," the man told Mr. Brown. "Relax. I don't believe in preparing a speech. Nope, preparation's no good. Spoils the charm of the thing; kills gaiety. I just wait for the inspiration to come to me when I'm on my feet—and it never fails."

These reassuring words let Mr. Brown look forward to a fine introduction, he recalls in his book, *Accustomed As I Am*. But when the man arose to make it, it came out this way:

Gentlemen, may I have your attention, please? We have bad news for you tonight. We wanted to have Isaac F Marcosson speak to you, but he couldn't come. He's sick. (Applause.) Next we asked Senator Bledridge to address you...but he was busy. (Applause.) Finally we tried in vain to get Doctor Lloyd Grogan of Kansas City to come down to speak to you. (Applause.) So, instead, we have—John Mason Brown. (Silence.)

Mr. Brown, recalling this disaster, said only: "At least my friend, that inspirationalist, got my name correctly."

Of course you can see that this man, who was so sure his inspiration would carry him through, couldn't have done much worse if he had tried to do so. His introduction violated every obligation he had both to the speaker whom he was introducing and to the audience which was to hear the speaker. There aren't many of these obligations, but they are important, and it is astonishing how many program chairmen fail to realize this.

The speech of introduction serves the same purpose as a social introduction. It brings the speaker and the audience wgether, establishes a friendly atmosphere, and creates a bond of interest between them. The man who says, "You don't have to make a speech, all you have to do is introduce the speaker," is guilty of understatement. No speech is more mangled than the speech of introduction, probably because it is looked upon as unimportant by many chairmen who are entrusted with the duty of preparing and delivering it.

An introduction—that term was fashioned from two Latin words, *intro,* to the inside, and *ducere,* to lead—ought to lead us to the inside of the topic sufficiently to make us want to hear it discussed. It ought to lead us to the inside facts regarding the speaker, facts that demonstrate his fitness for discussing this particular topic. In other words, an introduction ought to "sell" the topic to the audience and it ought to "sell" the speaker. And it ought to do these things in the briefest amount of time possible.

That is what it ought to do. But does it? Nine times out of ten, no—emphatically *no.* Most introductions are poor affairs, feeble and inexcusably inadequate. They do not have to be. If the speaker making the introduction realizes the importance of his task and goes about doing it in the right way he will soon be in demand as a chairman or master of ceremonies.

Here are some suggestions to help you make a well organized speech of introduction.

FIRST

Thoroughly Prepare What You are Going to Say

Even though the introductory talk is short, hardly ever exceeding one minute, it demands careful preparation. First, you must gather your facts. These will center around three items: the subject of the speaker's talk, his qualifications to speak on that subject, and his name. Often a fourth item will become apparent—why the subject chosen by the speaker is of special interest to the audience.

Be certain that you know the correct title of the talk something about the speaker's development of the subject matter. There is nothing more embarrassing than for the speaker to take exception to the introduction by disclaiming part of it as untrue of his stand on the subject. This can be obviated by making sure you know what the speaker's subject is and refraining from trying to predict what he will say. But your duty as introducer demands that you give the title of the speaker's talk correctly and point out its relevancy to the audience's interests. If at all possible, try to get this information directly from the speaker. If you have to rely on a third party, a program chairman, for instance, try to get the information in writing and check with the speaker just before the meeting.

But perhaps most of your preparation will involve getting the facts on the speaker's qualifications. In some cases you will be able to get an accurate listing from *Who's Who* or a comparable work, if your speaker is nationally or regionally well known. On the local level you can appeal to the public relations or personnel office of the concern where he works, or in some cases verify your facts by calling a close friend or a member of his family. The main idea is to get your biographical facts correct. People close to your speaker will be glad to furnish you with material.

Of course, too many facts will become boring, especially when one degree implies the speaker's acquisition of lesser degrees. To say that a man received a B.S. and an M.A. degree is superfluous when you indicate that he is a Doctor of Philosophy. Likewise, it is best to indicate the highest and most recent offices a man has held rather than to string out a catalogue of the positions he has held since leaving college. Above all, do not pass over the most distinguished achievements of a man's career instead of the less important

For example, I heard a well-known speaker—a man who ought to have known better—introduce the Irish poet W. B. Yeats. Yeats was to read his own poetry. Three years prior to that he had been awarded the Nobel Prize in literature, the highest distinction that can be bestowed upon a man of letters. I am confident that not ten per cent of that particular audience knew of the award or its significance. Both ought, by all means, to have been mentioned. They ought to have been announced even if nothing else were said. But what did the chairman do? He utterly ignored these facts, and wandered off into talking about mythology and Greek poetry.

Above all, be certain of the speaker's name and begin at once to familiarize yourself with its pronunciation. John Mason Brown says that he has been introduced as John Brown Mason and even John Smith Mason. In his delightful essay, "We Have with Us Tonight," Stephen Leacock, the distinguished Canadian humorist, tells of one introduction he received in which the introducer said:

There are many of us who have awaited Mr. Learoyd's coming with the most pleasant anticipations. We seemed from his books to know him already as an old friend. In fact I do not think I exaggerate when I tell Mr. Learoyd that his name in our city has long been a household word. I have very, very great pleasure in introducing to you—Mr. Learoyd.

The main purpose of your research is to be specific, for only by being specific will the introduction achieve its purpose—to heighten the audience's attention and make it receptive to the speaker's talk. The chairman who comes to a meeting poorly prepared usually comes up with something as vague and soporific as this:

Our speaker is recognized everywhere as an authority on his subject. We are interested in hearing what he has to say on this subject, because he comes from a great distance. It gives me great pleasure to present, let's see now, oh, here it is, Mr. Blank.

By taking a little time to prepare we can avoid the sad impression such an introduction makes upon both speaker and audience.

SECOND

Follow the T-I-S Formula

For most introductions, the T-I-S formula serves as a handy guide in organizing the facts you have collected in your research:

T stands for Topic. Start your introduction by giving the exact title of the speaker's talk.

I stands for Importance. In this step you bridge over the area between the topic and the particular interests of the group.

S stands for Speaker. Here you list the speaker's outstanding qualifications, particularly those that relate to his topic. Finally, you give his name, distinctly and clearly.

There is plenty of room in this formula for using your imagination. The introduction need not be cut and dried. Here is an example of an introduction that follows the formula without giving the effect of a formula at all. It was given by a New York City editor, Homer Thorne, when he introduced a New York Telephone Company executive, George Wellbaum, to a group of newspaper men and women:

Our speaker's topic is "The Telephone Serves You."

It seems to me that one of the world's big mysteries—like love and a horse player's persistence—is the mystery of what happens when you make a telephone call.

Why do you get a wrong number? Why can you sometimes make a call from New York to Chicago quicker than from your own home town to another town just over the hill? Our speaker knows the answers, and all the others to telephone questions. For twenty years it has been his job to digest all sorts of details about the telephone business and to make this business clear to other people. He is a telephone company executive who has earned his title by work.

“He will speak to us now about the ways his company serves us. If you are feeling friendly toward the service today, look on him as a patron saint. If you’ve recently been annoyed by your telephone, let him be a spokesman for the defense.

Ladies and Gentlemen, the vice-president of the New York Telephone Company, Mr. George Wellbaum.

Notice how cleverly the introductory speaker gets the audience thinking about the telephone. By asking questions he excites their curiosity and then indicates that the speaker will answer these questions and any others the audience may have.

I doubt that this introduction was written out or memorized. Even on paper it sounds conversational and natural. An introduction should never be memorized. Cornelia Otis Skinner was once introduced by a chairman of the evening whose memorized words she forgot as she began. She took a deep breath and then said: “Due to the exorbitant price of Admiral Byrd, we have with us this evening, Miss Cornelia Otis Skinner.”

The introduction should be spontaneous, seemingly arising out of the occasion, not strait-laced and severe.

In the introduction of Mr. Wellbaum, quoted above, there are no cliches, such as, “it gives me great pleasure,’ and “it is a great privilege to introduce to you.” The best way to present a speaker is to give his name or to say, “I present,” and give his name.

Some chairmen are guilty of talking too long and making the audience restive. Others indulge in flights of oratorical fancy in order to impress the speaker and the audience with a sense of their importance. Still others make the sad error of dragging in "canned jokes," sometimes not in the best taste, or of using humor that patronizes or deprecates the speaker's profession. All of these faults should be avoided by the man who is desirous of achieving the purposes of an effective introduction.

Not many years ago it was a kind of oratorical fashion to over-praise the speaker in the introduction. Bouquets of flowers were heaped upon the speaker by the chairman. The poor speaker was often overwhelmed by the heavy odor of flattery.

A popular humorist, Tom Collins, of Kansas City, Missouri, told Herbert Prochnow, author of *The Toastmaster's Handbook,* that "it is fatal to a speaker who intends to be humorous to promise his audience they soon will be rolling in the aisles with uncontrollable mirth. When a toastmaster begins to mumble about Will Rogers, you know you might just as well cut your wrists and go home, because you are ruined."

On the other hand, don't under-praise either. Stephen Leacock recalls the time he had to respond to introductory remarks that ended in this manner:

This is the first of our series of lectures for this winter. The last series, as you all know, was not a success. In fact, we came out at the end of the year with a deficit. So this year we are starting a new line and trying the experiment of cheaper talent. May I present Mr. Leacock.

Mr. Leacock dryly comments: "Judge how it feels to crawl out in front of the audience labelled 'cheaper talent."'

THIRD

Be Enthusiastic

In making an introduction of a speaker, manner is quite as important as matter. You should try to be friendly. and instead of saying how happy you are, be genuinely pleasant making your talk. If you give the introduction with a sense of building to a climax at the end when you announce the speaker's name, the sense of anticipation will be increased and the audience will applaud the speaker more enthusiastically. This display of the audience's good feeling will in tum help to stimulate the speaker to do his best.

When you do pronounce the speaker's name at the very end of the introduction it is well to remember the words, "pause," "part," and "punch." By *pause* is meant that a little silence just before the name is given will give an edge to anticipation; by *part* is meant that the first and last names should be separated by a slight pause so that the audience gets a clear impression of the speaker's name; by *punch* is meant that the name should be given with vigor and force.

There is one more caution: please, I beg of you, when you do enunciate the speaker's name, don't turn to him. but look out over the audience until the last syllable has been uttered; *then* turn to the speaker. I have seen countless chairmen give fine introductory speeches that were ruined at the end because they turned toward the speaker, pronouncing his name for him alone and leaving the audience in total ignorance of his identity.

FOURTH

Be Warmly Sincere

Be sure to be sincere. Do not indulge in deprecatory remarks or snide humor. A tongue-in-cheek type of introduction is often misinterpreted by some members of the audience. Be warmly sincere, because you are in a social situation that demands the highest kind of finesse and tact. You may be on familiar terms with the speaker, but the audience isn't, and some of your remarks, innocent though they be, may be misconstrued.

FIFTH

Thoroughly Prepare the Talk of Presentation

"It has been proved that the deepest yearning of the human heart is for recognition—for honor!"

When Margery Wilson, the author, wrote this she expressed a universal feeling. We all want to get along well in life. We want to be appreciated. Someone else's commendation, if it is only a word—let alone a gift presented at a formal affair—lifts the spirit magically.

Althea Gibson, the tennis star, managed to get this "yearning of the human heart" most aptly into the title of her autobiography. She called it, *I Wanted To Be Somebody.*

When we make a speech of presentation, we reassure the recipient that he really is *somebody.* He has succeeded in a certain effort. He is deserving of honor. We have come together to pay him this honor. What we have to say should be brief but we should give it careful thought. It may not mean much to those who are used to receiving honors, but to others less fortunate it may be something to be remembered brightly all the rest of a lifetime.

We, therefore, should give serious consideration to our choice of words in presenting the honor. Here is a time-tested formula:

Tell why the award is made. Perhaps it is for long service, or for winning a contest, or for a single notable achievement. Explain this simply.

Tell something of the group's interest in the life and activities of the person to be honored.

Tell how much the award is deserved and how cordially the group feels toward the recipient.

Congratulate the recipient and convey everyone's good

wishes for the future.

Nothing is so essential to this little talk as sincerity. Everyone realizes this, perhaps without saying so. So if you have been chosen to make a speech of presentation, you as well as the recipient have been honored. Your associates know you can be trusted with the task that demands a heart as well as a head. This must not tempt you to make certain mistakes that some speakers make. They are mistakes concerned with exaggeration.

At a time such as this, it is easy to exaggerate someone's virtues far beyond their teal measure. If the award is deserved, we must say so, but we should not add words of over-praise. Exaggerated praise makes the recipient uncomfortable and it doesn't convince an audience which knows better.

We also should avoid exaggerating the importance of the gift itself. Instead of stressing its intrinsic value, we should emphasize the friendly sentiments of those who are giving it.

SIXTH

Express Your Sincere Feelings in the Talk of Acceptance

This should be even shorter than the speech of presentation. It certainly shouldn't be anything we have memorized: yet being ready to make it will be an advantage. If we know we are to be given a present, with a speech of presentation, we shouldn't be at a loss for words of acknowledgment that will be a credit to us.

Just to mumble, "thank you" and "greatest day in my life" and "most wonderful thing that ever happened to me," is not very good. Here, as in the speech of presentation, a danger of exaggeration lurks. "Greatest day" and "most wonderful thing" take in too much territory. You can express heartfelt gratitude better in more moderate terms. Here is a suggested format:

Give a warmly sincere "thank you" to the group.

Give credit to others who have helped you, your associates, employers, friends, or family.

Tell what the gift or award means to you. If it is wrapped, open it and display it. Tell the audience how useful or decorative it is and how you intend to use it.

End with another sincere expression of your gratitude.

In this chapter we have discussed three special types of talks, any one of which you may be called upon to give in the course of your work or your affiliation with some organization or club.

I urge you to follow these suggestions carefully when making any of these talks and you will have the satisfaction that comes from saying the right thing at the right time.

Oratory is the highest form of music.

—Agona Apell

Fear doesn't exist anywhere except in the mind.

—Dale Carnegie

Chapter 5

ORGANIZING THE LONGER TALK

No sane man would start to build a house without some sort of plan; but why will he begin to deliver a talk without the vaguest notion of what he wishes to accomplish?

A talk is a voyage with a purpose, and it must be charted. The man who starts nowhere, generally gets there.

I wish that I could paint this saying of Napoleon's in flaming letters of red a foot high over every doorway on the globe where students of effective speaking foregather: "The art of war is a science in which nothing succeeds which has not been calculated and thought out."

That is just as true of speaking as of shooting. But do speakers realize it—or, if they do, do they always act on it? They do not. Many a talk has just a trifle more plan and arrangement than a bowl of Irish stew.

What is the best and most effective arrangement for a given set of ideas? No one can say until he has studied them. It is always a new problem, an eternal question that every speaker must ask and answer himself again and again. No infallible rules can be given; but we can, at any rate, indicate the three major phases of the longer talk to get action: the attention step, the body, and conclusion. For each, there are some time-tested methods of developing each phase.

FIRST

Get Attention Immediately

I once asked Dr. Lynn Harold Hough, formerly president of Northwestern University, what was the most important fact his long experience as a speaker has taught him. After pondering a moment, he replied, "To get an arresting opening, something that will seize favorable attention immediately." Dr. Hough struck at the heart of the matter of all persuasive speaking: how to get the audience 'tuned in' right from the speaker's first words. Here are some methods which, if applied, will give high attention value to your opening phrases.

BEGIN YOUR TALK WITH AN INCIDENT

Lowell Thomas, who has made a world-wide reputation as a news analyst, lecturer, and motion picture producer, began a talk on Lawrence of Arabia with this statement:

I was going down Christian Street in Jerusalem one day when I met a man clad in the gorgeous robes of an oriental potentate. At his side hung the curved gold sword worn only by the descendants of the prophet Mohammed...

And he was off—off with a *story* from *his experience.* That is what hooks attention. That kind of opening is almost foolproof. It can hardly fail. It moves, it marches. We follow because we identify ourselves as part of a situation and we want to know what is going to happen. I know of no more compelling method of opening a talk than by the use of a story. One of my own talks which I have given many times begins with these words:

Just after I had finished college, I was walking one night down a street in Huron, South Dakota, and I saw a man standing on a box talking to a crowd of people. I was curious, so I became part of the group listening to him. "Do you know," the speaker was saying, "that you never see a baldheaded Indian? Or you never see a bald-headed woman, do you? Now, I'm going to tell you why...."

No stalling. No "warm-up" statements. By launching directly into an incident, you can make it easy to capture an audience's attention.

A speaker who begins a talk with a story from his experience is on safe ground, for there is no groping for words, no loss of ideas. The experience he is relating is his, a re-creation, as it were, of part of his life, the very fiber of his being. The result? A self-assured, relaxed manner which will help a speaker establish himself on a friendly basis with an audience.

AROUSE SUSPENSE

Here is the way Mr. Powell Healy began a talk at the Penn Athletic Club in Philadelphia:

Eighty-two years ago, there was published in London a little volume, a story, which was destined to become immortal. Many people have called it "the greatest little book in the world" When it first appeared, friends meeting one another on the Strand or Pall Mall asked the question, "Have you read it?" The answer invariably was:

"Yes, God bless him, I have."

The day it was published a thousand copies were sold. Within a fortnight the demand had consumed fifteen thousand. Since then it has run into countless thousands of editions and has been translated into every language under heaven. A few years ago, J.P. Morgan purchased the original manuscript for a fabulous sum and it now reposes among the priceless treasures in his magnificent art gallery. What is this world famous book? It is.. .

Are you interested? Are you eager to know more? Has the speaker captured the favorable attention of his listeners? Do you feel this opening has held your attention, heightened your interest as it progressed? Why? Because it aroused your curiosity and held you in suspense.

Curiosity! Who is not susceptible to it?

Perhaps you, too! You are asking just who *is* the author and what is the book mentioned above? To satisfy your curiosity, here is the answer: The author: Charles Dickens, the book: *A Christmas Carol.*

Creating suspense is a sure-fire method of getting your listeners interested. Here is how I try to arouse suspense in my lecture on "How to Stop Worrying and Start Living." I begin like this: "In the spring of 1871, a young man who was destined to become a world-famous physician, William Osler, picked up a book and read twenty-one words that had a profound effect upon his future."

What were the twenty-one words? And how did these words affect his future? These are the questions your listeners will want answered.

STATE AN ARRESTING FACT

Clifford R. Adams, director of the Marriage Counseling Service of the Pennsylvania State College, began an article in *The Reader's Digest,* entitled "How to Pick a Mate," with these startling facts—facts that make you gasp, facts that make an arresting opener:

Today the chances that our young people will find happiness through marriage are slim indeed. The rise of our divorce rate is frightening. One marriage in five or six landed on the rocks in 1940. By 1946, it is expected to be one in four. And if long-range trends continue, the rate in fifty years will be one in two.

Here are two other examples of "arresting facts" openers:

"The War Department predicts that, in the first night of an atomic war, twenty million Americans will be killed."

"A few years ago, the Scripps-Howard newspapers spent $176,000 on a survey to discover what customers disliked about retail stores. It was the most costly, the most scientific, the most thorough survey ever made of retail selling problems. Questionnaires were sent into 54,047 homes in sixteen different cities. One of the questions was: What do you dislike about the stores in this town?'

"Almost two-fifths of all the answers to that question were the same: Discourteous clerks!"

This method of making startling statements at the beginning of a talk is effective in establishing contact the listener because it jars the mind. It is a kind of "shock technique" that enlists attention by using the unexpected to focus attention upon the subject matter of the talk.

One of our class members in Washington, D. C., used this method, arousal of curiosity, as effectively as anyone I have ever heard. Her name, Meg Sheil. Here is her opening:

"I was a prisoner for ten years. Not in an ordinary prison, but in one whose walls were worry about my inferiority and whose bars were the fear of criticism." Don't you want to know more about this true-life episode?

A danger of the startling opener must be avoided, that is, the tendency to be over-dramatic or too sensational. I remember one speaker who started his talk by shooting a pistol into the air. He got attention all right, but he also blasted the eardrums of his listeners.

Make your opening conversational in manner. An efficient way to discover whether you have an opener that is conversational is to try it out across the dinner table. If the way you open your talk isn't conversational enough to be spoken across the dinner table, it probably won't be conversational enough for an audience either.

Frequently, however, the opening of the talk that is supposed to get the listeners' interest is, in reality, the dullest part of the talk. For example, I recently heard a speaker begin like this: "Trust in the Lord and have faith in your own ability..." A preachy, obvious way to begin a talk! But note his second sentence; it is interesting; it has heart throb in it. "My mother was left a widow in 1918 with three children to support, and no money..." Why, oh *why,* didn't that speaker begin in his first sentence by telling about the struggles of his widowed mother with three little children to support!

If you want to interest your listeners, don't begin with an introduction. Begin by leaping right into the heart of your story.

That is what Frank Bettger does. He is the author of *How I Raised Myself From Failure to Success in Selling*. He is an artist when it comes to creating suspense in his first sentence. I know, because he and I traveled together all over the United States giving talks on selling under the auspices of the United States Junior Chamber of Commerce. I always admired the superb way he opened his talk on enthusiasm. No preaching. No lecturing. No sermonizing. No general statements. Frank Bettger leaped right into the heart of his subject in his first sentence. He began his talk on enthusiasm like this:

"Shortly after I started out as a professional baseball player, I got one of the biggest shocks of my life."

What effect did this opening have on his audience? I know, I was there. I saw the reaction. He had everyone's attention instantly. Everyone was eager to hear why and how he was shocked, and what he did about it.

ASK FOR A SHOW OF HANDS

A splendid way to get interested attention is to ask the audience to raise their hands in answer to a question. For example, I have opened my talk on "How to Prevent Fatigue" with this question:

"Let's see your hands. How many of you get tired more quickly than you feel you ought to?"

Note this point: When you ask for a show of hands, usually give the audience some warning that you are going to do so. Do not open a talk with: "How many people here believe the income tax should be lowered? Let's see your hands." Give the audience a chance to be ready for the vote by saying, for instance: "I am going to ask for a show of hands on a question of importance to you. This is the question: 'How many of you believe that trading stamps benefit the consumer?' "

The technique of asking for a show of hands gets a priceless reaction known as "audience participation." When you use it, your talk is no longer a one-sided affair. The audience is participating in it now. When you ask, "How many of you get tired more quickly than you feel you ought to?" everyone starts thinking of his favorite topic: himself, his aches, his fatigue. He lifts his hand and possibly looks around to see who else has his hand up. He forgets that he is listening to a talk. He smiles. He nods to a friend sitting next to him. The ice is broken. You, the speaker, are at ease, and so is the audience.

PROMISE TO TELL THE AUDIENCE HOW THEY CAN GET SOMETHING THEY WANT

An almost unfailing way to get alert attention is to promise to tell your listeners how they can get what they want by doing what you suggest. Following are some illustrations of what I mean:

"I am going to tell you how to prevent fatigue. I am going to tell you how to add one hour a day to your waking life."

"I'm going to tell you how you can materially increase your income."

"I promise that, if you will listen to me for ten minutes, I'll tell you one sure way to make yourself more popular."

The "promise" type of opener is sure to get attention because it goes straight to the self-interests of the audience. All too often speakers neglect to tie their topics to the vital interests of their hearers. Instead of opening the door to attention, they slam it shut with dull openings that trace the history of the subject matter or laboriously dwell upon the background necessary to an understanding of the topic.

I remember one talk I heard a few years ago on a topic which, in itself, was important to the audience: the necessity of periodic health examinations. How did the speaker begin his talk? Did he add to the natural attractiveness of his subject by an effective opening? No. He started with a colorless recital of the history of his topic and the audience began to lose interest in him and in his subject. An opening built around the "promise" technique would have been admirably appropriate. For instance:

Do you know how long you are expected to live? Life insurance companies can predict this by means of life expectancy tables which have been compiled from the lives of millions of persons. You can expect to live two-thirds of the time between your present age and eighty... now, is this long enough for you to live? No, no! We are all passionately eager to live longer and we want to prove that this prediction is wrong. But how, you ask, can this be done? How can I extend my life beyond the shockingly small number of years statisticians say remain for me? Well, there is an answer, a possible way this can be done, and I shall tell you how to do this...

I leave it to you to decide whether this type of opening captures your interest, if it compels you to listen to the speaker. You *must* listen to him because he not only is talking about you, about your life, but he has promised to tell you something of the most intense personal value to you. No dull recital of impersonal facts here! Such an opening as this is almost impossible to resist.

USE AN EXHIBIT

Perhaps the easiest way in the world to gain attention is to hold up something for people to look at. Almost any creature, from the simplest to the most complex, will give heed to that kind of stimulus. It can be used sometimes with effectiveness before the most dignified audience. For example, Mr. S. S. Ellis, of Philadelphia, opened one of his talks in one of our classes by holding a coin between his thumb and forefinger, and high above his shoulder. Naturally everyone looked. Then he inquired: "Has anyone here ever found a coin like this on the sidewalk? It announces that the fortunate finder will be given a lot free in such and such a real estate development. He has but to call and present this coin...." Mr. Ellis then proceeded to condemn the misleading and unethical practices involved.

All of the foregoing methods are commendable. They may be used separately or they may be combined. Recognize that how you open a talk largely determines whether the audience is going to accept you and your message.

SECOND

Avoid Getting Unfavorable Attention

Please, please, I urge you, remember that you must not only capture the attention of your audience, but you must capture their *favorable* attention. Please note that I said *favorable* attention. No rational person would begin a talk by insulting his audience or by making any obnoxious or disagreeable statement that would turn them against him and his message. Yet how frequently speakers begin talks by attracting attention through the use of-one of the following devices.

DO NOT OPEN WITH AN APOLOGY

To begin a talk with an apology does not get you off to a good start either. How often we all have heard speakers begin by calling the attention of the audience to their lack of preparation or their lack of ability. If you are not prepared, the audience will probably discover it without your assistance. Why insult your audience by suggesting that you did not think them worth preparing for, that just any old thing you had on the fire was good enough to serve them? No, we don't want to hear apologies; we want to be informed and interested—to be *interested:* remember that. Let your opening sentence capture the interest of your audience. Not the second sentence. Not the third sentence. The *first!*

AVOID THE "FUNNY" STORY OPENING

You may have noticed that there is one method of opening a talk, and one much favored by speakers, that is not recommended here: the so-called "funny" story opening. For some lamentable reason, the novice feels that he ought to "lighten up" his talk by telling a joke; he assumes that the mantel of Mark Twain has descended upon his shoulders. Do not fall into this trap; you will discover to your embarrassment the painful truth that the "funny" story is more often pathetic than funny—and the story may be known to persons in your audience.

A sense of humor, though, is a prized asset for any speaker. A talk need not begin, nor be, heavy-footed, elephantine, and excessively solemn. Not at all. If you have the ability to tickle the risibilities of your audience by some witty reference to a local situaiimi in to sonic-L'-g arising out of the occasion or the remarks of a previous speaker, then by all means do so. Observe some incongruity. Exaggerate it. That type of humor is more likely to succeed than stale jokes about Pat and Mike, or mothers-in-law, or shaggy dogs, because it is *relevant* and because it is original.

Perhaps the easiest way to create merriment is to tell a story on yourself. Depict yourself in some ridiculous and embarrassing situation. That gets down to the very essence of humor. Jack Benny has used this device for years. He was one of the first major radio comedians to "poke fun" at himself. By making himself the butt of jokes concerning his ability to play the violin, his miserliness, and his age, Jack Benny works a rich vein of humor that keeps his ratings high from year to year.

Audiences open their hearts, as well as their minds, to speakers who deliberately deflate themselves by calling attention to some deficiency or failing on their part, in a humorous sense, of course. On the other hand, creating the image of the "stuffed shirt" or the visiting expert with all the answers leaves an audience cold and unreceptive.

THIRD

Support Your Main Ideas

In the longer talk to get action you will have several points; the fewer the better, but all of them will require support material. In Chapter Seven we discussed one method of supporting the point of a talk, which is what you want the audience to do, by illustrating it with a story, an experience out of your life. This type of example is popular because it appeals to a basic drive in people, summed up by the slogan, "Everybody Loves a Story." An incident or happening is the kind of example most often used by the average speaker, but it is by no means the only way your point can be supported. You might also use statistics, which are nothing more than illustrations scientifically grouped, expert testimony, analogies, exhibits, or demonstrations.

USE STATISTICS

Statistics are used to show the proportion of instances of a certain kind. They can be impressive and convincing, especially as evidence where an isolated example might not do as well. The effectiveness of the Salk anti-poliomyelitis vaccine program was measured by statistics gathered in all parts of the country. Isolated cases of ineffectiveness were the exceptions that proved the rule. A talk based on one of these exceptions would not, therefore, convince a parent that the Salk vaccine program would not protect his child.

Statistics, of themselves, can be boring. They should be judiciously used, and when used they should be clothed in a language that makes them vivid and graphic.

Here is an example of how statistics can be impressive by comparing them with things familiar to us. In backing up his point that a vast amount of time is lost by New Yorkers' neglecting to answer telephones promptly an executive said:

Out of each one hundred telephone connections made, seven show a delay of more than a minute before the person called answers. Every day 280,000 minutes are lost in this way. In the course of six months, this minute delay in New York is about equal to all the business days that have elapsed since Columbus discovered America.

Mere numbers and amounts, taken by themselves, are never very impressive. They have to be illustrated; they ought, if possible, to be put in terms of our experiences. I remember listening to a lecture by a guide in the vast power room under Grand Coulee Dam. He could have given us the square-foot figures of the room's size, but that would not have been so convincing as the method he used. He told us that the room was large enough for a crowd of 10,000 people to view a football game on a regulation field and, in addition, there would be room left over for several tennis courts at each end!

Many years ago, a student in my course at the Brooklyn Central YMCA told in a talk the number of houses destroyed by fire during the previous year. He further said that, if these burned buildings had been placed side by side, the line would have reached from New York to Chicago, and that if the people who had been killed in those fires had been placed half a mile apart, that gruesome line would reach back again from Chicago to Brooklyn.

The figures he gave I forgot almost immediately but years have passed, and, without any effort on my part, I can still see that line of burning buildings stretching from Manhattan Island to Cook County, Illinois.

USE THE TESTIMONY OF EXPERTS

Frequently you can effectively back up the points you want to make in the body of your talk by the use of the testimony of an expert. Before using testimony it should be tested by answering these questions:

Is the quotation I am about to use accurate?

Is it taken from the area of the man's expert knowledge? To quote Joe Louis on economics would obviously be exploiting his name but not his forte.

Is the quotation from a man who is known and respected by the audience?

Are you sure that the statement is based on firsthand knowledge, not personal interest or prejudice?

USE ANALOGIES

An analogy, according to Webster, is a "relation of likeness between two things...consisting in the resemblance not of the things themselves but of two or more attributes, circumstances, or effects."

The use of an analogy is a fine technique for supporting a main idea. Here is an excerpt from a talk on "The Need for More Electric Power," by C. Girard Davidson when he was Assistant Secretary of the Interior. Note how he employs a comparison, all analogy, to back up his point:

A prosperous economy has to keep moving forward or it goes into a tailspin. There is a parallel with the airplane, which is a useless collection of nuts and bolts standing still on the ground. When moving forward in the air, however, it comes into its own and serves as a useful function. To stay up, it has to keep going forward. If it doesn't move, it sinks—and it can't move backward.

Here is another, perhaps one of the most outstanding analogies in the history of eloquence; it was used by Lincoln in answer to his critics during a crucial period of the Civil War:

Gentlemen, I want you to suppose a case for a moment. Suppose that all the property you were worth was in gold, and you had put it in the hands of Blondin, the famous rope-walker, to carry across the Niagara Falls on a tightrope. Would you shake the rope while he was passing over it, or keep shouting to him, "Blondin, stoop a little more! Go a little faster!" No, I am sure you would not. You would hold your breath as well as your tongue, and keep your hands off until he was safely over. Now the government is in the same situation. It is carrying an immense weight across a stormy ocean. Untold treasures are in its hands. It is doing the best it can. Don't badger it! Just keep still, and it will get you safely over.

USE A DEMONSTRATION WITH OR WITHOUT AN EXHIBIT

When executives of the Iron Fireman firm were talking to dealers, they needed some way of dramatizing the fact that fuel should be fed into a furnace from the bottom rather than from the top. So they hit on this simple but striking demonstration. The speaker lights a candle. Then he says:

See how clearly the flame burns—how tall it is. Since virtually all the fuel is being converted into heat, it gives off practically no smoke.

The fuel of the candle is fed in from below, just as the Iron Fireman feeds fuel into a furnace. Suppose that this candle was fueled from above, as hand-stoked furnaces are. *(Here the speaker turns the candle upside down.)*

Notice how the flame dies down. Smell the smoke. Hear it sputter. See how red the flame is because of incomplete combustion. And finally the flame goes out, as a result of inefficient fueling from above.

Some years ago, Henry Morton Robinson wrote an interesting article on "How Lawyers Win Cases" for *Your Life* magazine. In it, he describes how a lawyer named Abe Hummer is credited with a telling dramatic demonstration of showmanship while representing an insurance company in a damage suit. The plaintiff, a Mr. Postlethwaite, stated that as a result of falling down an elevator shaft his shoulder had been so severely injured that he was unable to raise his right arm.

Hummer appeared to be gravely concerned. "Now Mr. Postlethwaite," he said confidently, "show the jury how high you can raise your arm." Gingerly, Postlethwaite brought his arm up to ear level. "Now show us how high you could raise it before you were injured," urged Hummer. "As high as this," said the plaintiff, shooting his arm at full length over his head.

You may draw your own conclusion regarding the reaction of the jury to this demonstration.

In the longer talk to secure action you might make three, or at most, four points. They could be uttered in less than a minute. To recite them to an audience would be dull and boring. What makes these points come alive? It is the support material you use. This is what gives sparkle and interest to your talk. By the use of incidents, comparisons and demonstrations, you make your main ideas clear and vivid; by the use of statistics and testimony you substantiate the truth and emphasize the importance of your main points.

FOURTH

Appeal for Action

I dropped in to talk a few minutes one day with George F. Johnson, the industrialist and humanitarian. He was President of the great Endicott-Johnson Corporation at the time. More interesting to me, though, was the knowledge that he was a speaker who could make his hearers laugh, and sometimes cry, and often remember for a long time what he said.

He didn't have a private office. He had a corner of a big, busy factory, and his manner was as unpretentious as his old wooden desk.

"You've come at a good time," he said as he stood up to

greet me. "I've just got a job out of the way. I've jotted down what I want to say at the end of a talk I'm going to give to the workers tonight."

"It's always a relief to get a talk ship-shape in your mind from beginning to end," I told him.

"Oh, I haven't got it all in mind yet," he said. "Just the general idea and the specific way I want to finish it."

He was not a professional speaker. He never went in for ringing words or fine phrases. From experience, however, he had learned one of the secrets of successful communication. He knew that if a talk is to go over well, it has to have a good ending. He realized that the conclusion of a talk is the part toward which all that precedes it must reasonably move if an audience is to be impressed.

The close is really the most strategic point in a talk, what one says last, the final words left ringing in the ears when one ceases—these are likely to be remembered longest. Unlike Mr. Johnson, beginners seldom appreciate the importance of this; their endings often leave much to be desired.

What are their most common errors? Let us discuss a few and search for remedies.

First, there is the man who finishes with: "That is about all I have to say on the matter, so I guess I shall stop." This speaker usually throws a smoke screen over his inability to end a talk satisfactorily by lamely saying "thank you." That is not an ending. That is a mistake. It reeks of the amateur. That is almost unpardonable. If that is all you have to say, why not round off your talk, and promptly take your seat and stop without talking about stopping. Do that, and the inference that that is all you have to say may, with safety and good taste, be left to the discernment of the audience.

Then, there is the speaker who says all he has to say, but

he does not know how to stop. I believe it was Josh Billings who advised people to take the bull by the tail instead of the horns, since it would be easier to let go. This speaker has the bull by the frontal extremities, and wants to part company with him, but try as hard as he will, he can't get near a friendly fence or tree. So he finally thrashes about in a circle, covering the same ground, repeating himself, leaving a bad impression....

The remedy? An ending has to be planned sometime, doesn't it? Is it the part of wisdom to try to do it after you are facing an audience, while you are under the strain and stress of talking, while your mind must be intent on what you are saying? Or does common sense suggest the advisability of doing it quietly, calmly, beforehand?

How do you go about bringing your talk to a climactic close? Here are a few suggestions:

SUMMARIZE

In the longer talk a speaker is very apt to cover so much ground that at the close the listeners are a little hazy about all his main points. However, few speakers realize that. They are misled into assuming that because these points are crystal clear in their own minds, they must be equally lucid to their hearers. Not at all. The speaker has been pondering over his ideas for some time. But his points are all new to the audience; they are flung at the audience like a handful of shot. Some may stick, but most are liable to roll off in confusion. The hearers are liable, in the words of Shakespeare, to "remember a mass of things but nothing distinctly."

Here is a good example. The speaker, a traffic manager for one of Chicago's railways, ends his talk with this summary:

In short, gentlemen, our own back-door yard experience

with this block device; the experience in its use in the East, in the West, in the North; the sound operating principles underlying its operation; the actual demonstration in the money saved in one year in wreck prevention—move me most earnestly and unequivocally to recommend its immediate installation on our Southern branch.

You see what he has done? You can see it and feel it without having heard the rest of the talk. He has summed up in a few sentences, in sixty-two words, practically all the points he had made in the entire talk.

Don't you feel that a summary like that helps? If so, make that technique your own.

ASK FOR ACTION

The closing just quoted is also an excellent illustration of the ask-for-action ending. The speaker wanted something done: a block device installed on the Southern branch of his road. He based his request for action on the money it would save, on the wrecks it would prevent. The speaker wanted action, and he got it. This was not a mere practice talk. It was delivered before the board of directors of a railway, and it secured the installation of the block device for which it asked.

In your final words of a talk to secure action the time has come to ask for the order. So ask for it! Tell your audience to join, contribute, vote, write, telephone, buy, boycott, enlist, investigate, acquit, or whatever it is you want them to do. Be sure to obey these caution signs, however:

Ask them to do something specific. Don't say, "Help the Red Cross." That's too general. Say, instead, "Send your enrollment fee of one dollar tonight to the American Red Cross, 125 Smith Street in this city."

Ask the audience for some response that is within their

power to give. Don't say, "Let us cast our ballot against the Demon Rum." It can't be done. At the moment, we aren't ballotting on the Demon Rum. You could, instead, ask them to join a temperance society or to contribute to some organization which is fighting for prohibition.

Make it as easy as you can for your audience to act on your appeal. Don't say, "Write your congressman to vote against this bill." Ninety-nine per cent of your listeners won't do it. They are not vitally interested; or it is too much trouble; or they will forget. So make it easy and pleasant to act. How? By writing a letter yourself to your congressman, saying, "We, the undersigned, urge you to vote against Bill No. 74321." Pass the letter around with a fountain pen, and you will probably get a lot of signers—and perhaps lose your fountain pen.

> *90% of how well the talk will go is determined before the speaker steps on the platform.*
>
> *—Somers White*

> *Only the prepared speaker deserves to be confident.*
>
> *—Dale Carnegie*

Chapter 6

APPLYING WHAT YOU HAVE LEARNED

At the fourteenth session of my course I have often heard with pleasure students tell how they used the techniques in this book in their everyday lives. Salesmen point to increased sales, managers to promotions, executives to a widened span of control, all due to the increased skill with which they gave instructions and solved problems using the tools of effective speech.

As N. Richard Diller wrote in *Today's Speech:* "Talk, the type of talk, the amount of talk, and the atmosphere for such talk can act as the very life blood of an industrial communication system." R. Fred Canaday, in charge of the General Motors Dale Carnegie Course in Effective Leadership, wrote in the same magazine: "One of the basic reasons we at General Motors are interested in speech training is our recognition that every supervisor is a teacher to a greater or lesser degree. From the time he interviews a prospective employee, through the orientation phase of early employment, on through regular assignment and poccihle promotion, a supervisor is continually called upon to explain, describe, reprimand, inform, instruct, review, and discuss myriads of subjects with each person in his department."

As we proceed up the ladder of oral communication to those areas that come closest to public speaking—discussions, decision-making, problem-solving and policy-formulating conferences—we see again how the skills of effective speaking as taught in this book can be transferred to everyday speech activities. The rules for effective speaking before groups are directly applicable to conference participation and conference leadership.

Organization of the idea to be presented, the choice of the right words to launch it, the earnestness and enthusiasm used in delivering it are elements that will guarantee the idea's life in the final stage of solution. All these elements have been thoroughly discussed in this book. It remains for the reader to apply what he has learned in every conference in which he participates.

Perhaps you are wondering when to begin applying what you have learned in the previous thirteen chapters of this book. You may be surprised if I answer that query by one word: Immediately.

Even though you are not planning to make a speech in public for some time, if at all, I am certain you will find that the principles and techniques in this book are applicable every day. When I say start using these techniques *now,* I mean in the very next speaking situation in which you find yourself.

If you analyze the speaking that you do every day, you will be amazed by the similarity of purpose between your daily speaking and the type of formal communication discussed in these pages.

In Chapter Seven, you were urged to keep in mind one of

four general purposes when you speak before groups; you may want to give them information, entertain them, convince them that your position is right, or persuade them to take action of some kind. In public speaking we try to keep these purposes distinct, both as to the content of the talk and the manner of our delivery.

In daily speaking, these purposes are fluid, merging with one another and constantly changing through the course of the day. At one moment we may be indulging in friendly chitchat and then suddenly we may be using speech to sell a product or persuade a child to put his spending money in the bank. By applying the techniques described in this book to everyday conversation we can make ourselves more effective, get our ideas across more efficiently, and motivate others with skill and fact.

FIRST

Use Specific Detail in Everyday Conversation

Take just one of these techniques, for instance. Remember in Chapter Four I appealed to you to put detail in your talk. In that way you make your ideas come alive, in a vivid and graphic way. Of course I was thinking mainly of speaking before groups. But isn't the use of detail just as important in everyday conversation? Just think for a moment of the really interesting conversationalists of your acquaintance. Aren't they the ones who fill their talk with colorful, dramatic details, who have the ability to use picturesque speech?

Before you can begin to develop your conversational skills you must have confidence. So almost all that was said in the first three chapters of this book will be useful in giving you the security to mix with others and to voice your opinions in an informal social group. Once you are eager to express your ideas even on a limited scale, you will begin to search your experience for material that can be converted to conversation. Here a wonderful thing happens—your horizons begin to expand and you see your life take on new meaning.

Housewives, whose interests may have become somewhat restricted, have been most enthusiastic in reporting what happens when they begin to apply their knowledge of speaking techniques to small conversational groups. "I realize that my newly found confidence gave me courage to speak up at social functions," Mrs. R. D. Hart told her classmates in Cincinnati, "and I began taking an interest in current events. Instead of withdrawing from the give and take of the group I eagerly joined it. Not only that, but everything I did became grist for the conversational mill and I found myself becoming interested in a host of new activities."

To an educator there is nothing new in Mrs. Hart's grateful report. Once the drive to learn and to apply what has been learned is stimulated, it starts a whole train of action and interaction that vivifies the entire personality. A cycle of achievement is set up and, like Mrs. Hart, one gets the feeling of fulfillment, all through putting into practice just one of the principles taught in this book.

Though few of us are professional teachers, all of us use speech to inform others on many occasions during the day. As parents instructing our children, as neighbors explaining a new method of pruning roses, as tourists exchanging ideas on the best route to follow, we constantly find ourselves in conversational situations that require clarity and coherence of thought, vitality and vigor expression. What was said in Chapter Eight in relation to the talk to inform is applicable in these situations as well.

SECOND

Use Effective Speaking Techniques in Your Job

Now we enter the area of the communicative process as it affects our jobs. As salesmen, managers, clerks, department heads, group leaders, teachers, ministers, nurses, executives, doctors, lawyers, accountants, and engineers. we are all charged with the responsibility of explaining specialized areas of knowledge and giving professional instructions. Our ability to make these instructions in clear, concise language may often be the yardstick used by our superiors in judging our competence. How to think quickly and verbalize adroitly is a skill acquired in presenting speeches of information, but this skill is by no means limited to formal speaking—it can be used every day by every one of us. The need for clarity in business and professional speech today is highlighted by the recent spate of oral communications courses in industry, government, and professional organizations.

THIRD

Seek Opportunities to Speak in Public

In addition to using the principles of this book in everyday speech, where incidentally you will reap the greatest rewards, you should seek every opportunity to speak in public. How do you do this? By joining a club where public speaking of some sort goes on. Don't just be an inactive member, a mere looker-on. Pitch in and help by doing committee work. Most of these jobs go begging. Get to be program chairman. That will give you an opportunity to interview good speakers in your community, and you certainly will be called upon to make speeches of introduction.

As soon as possible, develop a twenty to' thirty minute

talk. Use the suggestions in this book as a guide. Let your club or organization know that you are prepared to address them. Offer your services to a speaker's bureau in your town. Fund-raising campaigns are looking for volunteers to speak for them. They provide you with a speaker's kit which will be of great help in preparing your talk. Many speakers of consequence have begun in this way. Some of them have risen to great prominence. Take Sam Levenson, for example, the radio and TV star and a speaker whose services are sought all over the country. He was a high school teacher in New York. Just as a sideline he began making short talks about what he knew best, his family, relatives, his students, and the unusual aspects of his job. These talks took fire, and he was soon asked to address so many groups it began to interfere with his teaching chores. But, by this time he was a guest on network programs and it wasn't long before Sam Levenson transferred his talents entirely to the entertainment world.

FOURTH

You Must Persist

When we learn any new thing, like French or golf or speaking in public, we never advance steadily. We do not improve gradually. We do it by waves, by abrupt starts and sudden stops. Then we remain stationary a time, or we may even slip back and lose some of the ground we have previously gained. These periods of stagnation, or retrogression, are well known by all psychologists; they have been named "plateaus in the curve of learning." Students of effective speaking will sometimes be stalled, perhaps for weeks, on one of these plateaus. Work as hard as they may, they cannot seem to get off it. The weak ones give up in despair. Those with grit persist, and they find that suddenly, almost overnight, without knowing how or why it has happened, they have made great progress. They have lifted from the plateau like an airplane. Abruptly they have acquired naturalness, force, and confidence in their speaking.

You may always, as has been stated elsewhere in these pages, experience some fleeting fear, some shock, some nervous anxiety, the first few moments you face an audience. Even the greatest musicians have felt it in spite of their innumerable public appearances. Paderewski always fidgeted nervously with his cuffs immediately before he sat down at the piano. But as soon as he began to play, all of his audience-fear vanished quickly like a <u>mkt</u> in Auust surainc.

His experience will be yours. If you will but persevere, you will soon eradicate everything, including this initial fear; and that will be initial fear, and nothing more. After the first few sentences, you will have control of yourself. You will be speaking with positive pleasure.

One time a young man who aspired to study law wrote to Lincoln for advice. Lincoln replied: "If you are resolutely determined to make a lawyer of yourself, the thing is more than half done already.... Always bear in mind that your own resolution to succeed is more important than any other one thing."

Lincoln knew. He had gone through it all. He had never, in his entire life, had more than a total of one year's schooling. And books? Lincoln once said he had walked and borrowed every book within fifty miles of his home. A log fire was usually kept going all night in the cabin. Sometimes he read by the light of that fire. There were cracks between the logs in the cabin, and Lincoln often kept a book sticking there. As soon as it was light enough to read in the morning, he rolled over on his bed of leaves, rubbed his eyes, pulled out the book and began devouring it.

He walked twenty and thirty miles to hear a speaker and, returning home, he practiced his talks everywhere—in the fields, in the woods, before the crowds gathered at Jones' grocery at Gentryville; he joined literary and debating societies in New Salem and Springfield, and practiced speaking on the topics of the day. He was shy in the presence of women; when he courted Mary Todd he used to sit in the parlor, bashful and silent, unable to find words, listening while she did the talking. Yet that was the man who, by faithful practice and home study, made himself into the speaker who debated with the most accomplished orator of his day, Senator Douglas. This was the man who, at Gettysburg, and again in his second inaugural address, rose to heights of eloquence that have rarely been attained in all the annals of mankind.

Small wonder that, in view of his own terrific handicaps and pitiful struggle, Lincoln wrote: "If you are resolutely determined to make a lawyer out of yourself, the thing is more than half done already."

An excellent picture of Abraham Lincoln hangs in the President's office in the White House. "Often when I had some matter to decide," said Theodore Roosevelt, "something involved and difficult to dispose of, something where there were conflicting rights and interest, I would look up at Lincoln, try to imagine him in my place, try to figure out what he would do in the same circumstances. It may sound odd to you, but, frankly, it seemed to make my troubles easier of solution."

Why not try Roosevelt's plan? Why not, if you are discouraged and feeling like giving up the fight to make a more effective speaker of yourself, why not ask yourself what he would do under the circumstances? You know what he would do. You know what he did do. After he had been beaten by Stephen A. Douglas in the race for the U.S. Senate, he admonished his followers not to "give up after one or one hundred defeats."

FIFTH

Keep the Certainty of Reward Before You

How I wish I could get you to prop this book open on your breakfast table every morning until you had memorized these words from Professor William James:

Let no youth have any anxiety about the upshot of his education, whatever the line of it may be. If he keeps faithfully busy each hour of the working day, he may safely leave the final result to itself. He can, with perfect certainty, count on waking up some fine morning to find himself one of the competent ones of his generation, in whatever pursuit he may have singled out.

• • •

And now, with the renowned Professor James to fall back upon, I shall go so far as to say that if you keep right on practicing intelligently, you may confidently hope to wake up one fine morning and find yourself one of the competent speakers of your city or community.

Regardless of how fantastic that may sound to you now, *it is true as a general principle.* Exceptions, of course, there are. A man with an inferior mentality and personality, and with nothing to talk about, is not going to develop into a local Daniel Webster; but, *within reason,* the assertion is correct.

Let me illustrate: former Governor Stokes of New Jersey attended the closing banquet of one of our classes at Trenton. He remarked that the talks he had heard that evening were as good as the speeches that he had heard in the House of Representatives and Senate at Washington. These Trenton "speeches" were made by businessmen who had been tongue-tied with audience-fear a few months previously. They were not incipient Ciceros, these New

Jersey businessmen; they were typical of the businessmen one finds in any American city. Yet they woke up one fine morning to find themselves among the competent speakers of their city, and probably in the country.

I have known and carefully watched literally thousands of persons trying to gain self-confidence and the ability to talk in public. Those that succeeded were, in only a few instances, persons of unusual brilliancy. For the most part, they were the ordinary run of businessmen you will find in your own home town. But they kept on. More exceptional men sometimes got discouraged or too deeply immersed in money-making, and they did not get very far; but the ordinary individual with grit and singleness of purpose, at the end of the road, was at the top.

That is only human and natural. Don't you see the same tiling occurring all the time in commerce and the professions? John D. Rockefeller, Sr., said that the first essential for success in business was patience and the knowledge that reward is ultimately certain. It is likewise one of the first essentials for success in effective speaking.

A few summers ago, I started out to scale a peak in the Austrian Alps called the *Wilder Kaiser*. Baedaker said that the ascent was difficult, and a guide was essential for amateur climbers. A friend and I had none, and we were certainly amateur, so a third party asked us if we thought we were going to succeed. "Of course," we replied.

"What makes you think so?" he inquired.

"Others have done it without guides," I said, "so I know it is within reason, and *I never undertake anything thinking defeat.*"

That is the proper psychology for anything from speaking to an assault on Mt. Everest.

How well you succeed is largely determined by thoughts

you have prior to speaking. See yourself in your imagination talking to others with perfect selfcontrol.

It is easily in your power to do this. Believe that you will succeed. Believe it firmly, and you will then do what is necessary to bring success about.

During the Civil War, Admiral Dupont gave half a dozen excellent reasons why he had not taken his gunboat into Charleston harbor. Admiral Farragut listened Intently to the recital. "But there was another reason that you have not mentioned," he replied.

"What is that?" questioned Admiral Dupont.

The answer came: "You did not believe you could do it."

The most valuable thing that most members acquire from training in our classes is an increased confidence in themselves, an additional faith in their ability to achieve. What is more important for one's success in almost any undertaking?

Emerson wrote, "Nothing great was ever achieved without enthusiasm." That is more than a well-turned literary phrase; it is the road map to success.

William Lyon Phelps was probably the most beloved and the most popular professor ever to teach at Yale University. In his book *The Excitement of Teaching,* he states, "With me, teaching is more than an art or an occupation. It is a passion. I love to teach, as a painter loves to paint, as a singer loves to sing, as a poet loves to write. Before I get out of bed in the morning, I think with ardent delight of my group of students."

Is there any wonder a teacher so filled with enthusiasm for his job, so excited about the work ahead of him, achieved success? Billy Phelps exerted a tremendous influence on his students, largely by the love and excitement, by the enthusiasm, he put into his teaching.

If you put enthusiasm into learning how to speak more effectively you will find that the obstacles in your path will disappear. This is a challenge to focus all your talent and power on the goal of effective communication with your fellow men. Think of the self-reliance, the assurance, the poise that will be yours, the sense of mastery that comes from being able to hold the attention, stir the emotions, and convince a group to act. You will find that competence in self-expression will lead to competence in other ways as well, for training in effective speaking is the royal road to self-confidence in all the areas of working and living.

In the manual for the guidance of instructors who teach the Dale Carnegie Course are these words: "When class members discover that they can hold the attention of an audience and receive an instructor's praise, and the applause of the class—when they are able to do that, they develop a sense of inner power, courage, and calm that they have never before experienced. The result? They undertake and accomplish things that they never dreamed possible. They find themselves longing to talk before groups. They take active parts in business and professional and community activities, and become leaders."

The word "leadership" has been used often in the chapters that have gone before this one. Clear, forceful, and emphatic expressiveness is one of the marks of leadership in our society. This expressiveness must govern all the utterances of the leader from private interview to public pronouncements. Properly applied, the material in this book will help to develop leadership—in the family, the church group, the civic organization, the corporation, and the government.

The most precious things in speech are the pauses.

—Sir Ralph Richardson

Speakers who talk about what life has taught them never fail to keep the attention of their listeners.

—Dale Carnegie

PART III

THE THREE ASPECTS OF EVERY SPEECH

Chapter 7

EARNING THE RIGHT TO TALK

Many years ago, a Doctor of Philosophy and a rough-and-ready fellow who had spent his youth in the British Navy were enrolled in one of our classes in New York. The man with the degree was a college professor; the ex-tar was the proprietor of a small side-street trucking business. His talks were far better received by the class than those given by the professor. Why? The college man used beautiful English. He was urbane, cultured, refined. His talks were always logical and clear. But they lacked one essential—concreteness. They were vague and general. Not once did he illustrate a point with anything approaching a personal experience. His talks were usually nothing more than a series of abstract ideas held together by a thin string of logic.

On the other hand, the trucking firm proprietor's language was definite, concrete, and picturesque. He talked in terms of everyday facts. He gave us one point and then backed it up by telling us what happened to him in the course of his business. He described the people he had to deal with and the headaches of keeping up with regulations. The virility and freshness of his phraseology made his talks highly instructive and entertaining.

I cite this instance, not because it is typical of college professors or of men in the trucking business, but because it illustrates the attention-compelling power of rich, colorful details in a talk.

There are four ways to develop speech material that guarantees audience attention. If you follow these four steps in your preparation you will be well on the way to commanding the eager attention of your listeners.

FIRST

Limit Your Subject

Once you have selected your topic, the first step is to stake out the area you want to cover and stay strictly within those limits. Don't make the mistake of trying to cover the open range. One young man attempted to speak for two minutes on the subject of 'Athens from 500 B.C. to the Korean War." How utterly futile! He barely had gone beyond the founding of the city before he had to sit down, another victim of the compulsion to cover too much in one talk. This is an extreme example, I know; I have heard thousands of talks, less encompassing in scope, that failed to hold attention for the same reason—they covered far too many points. Why? Because it is impossible for the mind to attend to a monotonous series of factual pointc If your talk sounds like the World Almanac you will not be able to hold attention very long. Take a simple subject, like a trip to Yellowstone Park. In their eagerness to leave nothing out, most people have something to say about every scenic view in the Park. The audience is whisked from one point to another with dizzying speed. At the end, all that remains in the mind is a blur of waterfalls, mountains, and geysers. How much more memorable such a talk would be if the speaker limited himself to one aspect of the Park, the wildlife or the hot springs, for example. Then there would be time to develop the kind of pictorial detail that would make Yellowstone Park come alive in all its vivid color and variety.

This is true of any subject, whether it be salesmanship, baking cakes, tax exemptions, or ballistic missiles. You must limit and select before you begin, narrow your subject down to an area that will fit the time at your disposal.

In a short talk, less than five minutes in duration, all you can expect is to get one or two main points across. In a longer talk, up to thirty minutes, few speakers ever succeed if they try to cover more than four or five main ideas.

SECOND

Develop Reserve Power

It is far easier to give a talk that skims over the surface than to dig down for facts. But when you take the easy way you make little or no impression on the audience. After you have narrowed your subject, then the next step is to ask yourself questions that will deepen your understanding and prepare you to talk with authority on the topic you have chosen: "Why do I believe this? When did I ever see this point exemplified in real life? What precisely am I trying to prove? Exactly how did it happen?"

Questions like these call for answers that will give you reserve power, the power that makes people sit up and take notice. It was said of Luther Burbank, the botanical wizard, that he produced a million plant specimens to find one or two superlative ones. It is the same with a talk. Assemble a hundred thoughts around your theme, then discard ninety.

"I always try to get ten times as much information as I use, sometimes a hundred times as much," said John

Gunther not long ago. The author of the bestselling "Inside" books was speaking of the way he prepared to write a book or give a talk.

On one occasion in particular, his actions bore out his words. In 1956, he was working on a series of articles on mental hospitals. He visited institutions, talked to supervisors, attendants, and patients. A friend of mine was with him, giving some small assistance in the research, and he told me they must have walked countless miles up stairs and down, along corridors, building to building, day after day. Mr. Gunther filled notebooks. Back in his office, he stacked up government and state reports, private hospital reports, and reams of committees' statistics.

"In the end," my friend told me, "he wrote four short articles, simple enough and anecdotal enough to make good speeches. The paper on which they were typed weighed, perhaps, a few ounces. The filled notebooks, and everything else he used as the basis for the few ounces of product, must have weighed twenty pounds."

Mr. Gunther knew that he was working with pay dirt He knew he couldn't overlook any of it. An old hand at this sort of thing, he put his mind to it, and he sifted out the gold nuggets.

A surgeon friend of mine said: "I can teach you in ten minutes how to take out an appendix. But it will take me four years to teach you what to do if something goes wrong." So it is with speaking: Always prepare so that you are ready for any emergency, such as a change of emphasis because of a previous speaker's remarks, or a well-aimed question from the audience in the discussion period following your talk.

You, too, can acquire reserve power by selecting your topic as soon as possible. Don't put it off until a day or two before you have to speak. If you decide on the topic early you will have the inestimable advantage of having your subconscious mind working for you. At odd moments of the day when you are free from your work, you can explore your subject, refine the ideas you want to convey to your audience. Time ordinarily spent in reverie while you are driving home, waiting for a bus, or riding the subway, can be devoted to mulling over the subject matter of your talk. It is during this incubation period that flashes of insight will come, just because you have determined your topic far in advance and your mind subconsciously works over it.

Norman Thomas, a superb speaker who has commanded the respectful attention of audiences quite opposed to his political point of view, said: “If a speech is to be of any importance at all, the speaker should live with the theme or message, turning it over and over in his mind. He will be surprised at how many useful illustrations or ways of putting his case will come to him as he walks the street, or reads a newspaper, or gets ready for bed, or wakes up in the morning. Mediocre speaking very often is merely the inevitable and the appropriate reflection of mediocre thinking, and the consequence of imperfect acquaintance with the subject in hand.”

While you are involved in this process you will be under strong temptation to write your talk out, word for word. Try not to do this, for once you have set a pattern, you are likely to be satisfied with it, and you may cease to give it any mote constructive thought. In addition, there is the danger of memorizing the script. Mark Twain had this to say about such memorization: “Written things are not for speech; their form is literary; they are stiff, inflexible, and will not lend themselves to happy effective delivery with the tongue. Where their purpose is merely to entertain, not to instruct, they have to be limbered up, broken up, colloquialized, and turned into the common form of unpremeditated talk; otherwise they will bore the house—not entertain it.”

Charles F. Kettering, whose inventive genius sparked the growth of General Motors, was one of America's most renowned and heartwarming speakers. Asked if he ever wrote out any part or all of his talks, he replied: "What I have to say is, I believe, far too important to write down on paper. I prefer to write on my audience's mind, on their emotions, with every ounce of my being. A piece of paper cannot stand between me and those I want to impress."

THIRD

Fill Your Talk with Illustrations and Examples

In the *Art of Readable Writing,* Rudolf Flesch begins one of his chapters with this sentence: "Only stories are really readable." He then shows how this principle is used by *Time* and *Reader's Digest*. Almost every article in these top-circulation magazines either is written as pure narrative or is generously sprinkled with anecdotes. There is no denying the power of a story to hold attention in talking before groups as well as writing for magazines.

Norman Vincent Peale, whose sermons have been heard by millions on radio and television, says that his favorite form of supporting material in a talk is the illustration or example. He once told an interviewer from the *Quarterly Journal of Speech* that "the true example is the finest method I know of to make an idea clear, interesting, and persuasive. Usually, I use several examples to support each major point."

Readers of my books are soon aware of my use of the anecdote as a means of developing the main points of my message. The rules from *How to Win Friends and Influence People* can be listed on one and a half pages. The other two hundred and thirty pages of the book are filled with stories and illustrations to point up how others have used these rules with wholesome effect.

How can we acquire this most important technique of using illustrative material? There are five ways of doing this: Humanize, Personalize, Specify, Dramatize, and Visualize.

HUMANIZE YOUR TALK

I once asked a group of American businessmen in Paris to talk on "How to Succeed." Most of them merely listed lot of abstract qualities and gave preachments on the value of hard work, persistence, and ambition.

So I halted this class, and said something like this: "We don't want to be lectured to. No one enjoys that. Remember, you must be entertaining or we will pay no attention whatever to what you are saying. Also remember that one of the most interesting things in the world is sublimated, glorified gossip. So tell us the stories of two men you have known. Tell why one succeeded and why the other failed. We will gladly listen to that, remember it, and possibly profit by it."

There was a certain member of that course who invariably found it difficult to interest either himself or his audience. This night, however, he seized the human interest suggestion and told us of two of his classmates in college. One of them had been so conservative that he had bought shirts at the different stores in town, and made charts showing which ones laundered best, wore longest, and gave the most service per dollar invested. His mind was always on pennies; yet, when he was graduated—it was an engineering college—he had such a high opinion of his own importance that he was not willing to begin at the bottom and work his way up, as the other graduates were doing. Even when the third annual reunion of the class came, he was still making laundry charts of his shirts, while waiting for some extraordinarily good thing to come his way. It never came. A quarter of a century has passed since then, and this man, dissatisfied and soured on life, still holds a minor position.

The speaker then contrasted with this failure the story of one of his classmates who had surpassed all expectations. This particular chap was a good mixer. Everyone liked him. Although he was ambitious to do big things later, he started as a draftsman. But he was always on the lookout for opportunity. Plans were then being made for the New York World's Fair. He knew engineering talent would be needed there, so he resigned from his position in Philadelphia and moved to New York. There he formed a partnership and engaged immediately in the contracting business. They did considerable work for the telephone company, and this man was finally taken over by that concern at a large salary.

I have recorded here only the bare outline of what the speaker told. He made his talk interesting and illuminating with a score of amusing and human interest details. He talked on and on—this man who could not ordinarily find material for a three-minute speech—and he was surprised to learn, when he stopped, that he had held the floor on this occasion for ten minutes. The speech had been so interesting that it seemed short to everyone. It was his first real triumph.

Almost everyone can profit by this incident. The average speech would be far more appealing if it were rich with human interest stories. The speaker should attempt to make only a few points and to illustrate them with concrete cases. Such a method of speech building can hardly fail to get and hold attention.

Of course, the richest source of such human interest material is your own background. Don't hesitate to tell us about your experiences because of some feeling that you should not talk about yourself. The only time an audience objects to hearing a person talk about himself is when he does it in an offensive, egotistical way. Otherwise, audiences are tremendously interested in the personal stories speakers tell. They are the surest means of holding attention; don't neglect them.

PERSONALIZE YOUR TALK BY USING NAMES

By all means, when you tell stories involving others, use their names, or, if you want to protect their identity, use fictitious names. Even impersonal names like "Mr. Smith" or "Joe Brown" are far more descriptive than "this man" or "a person." The label identifies and individualizes. As Rudolf Flesch points out, "Nothing adds more realism to a story than names; nothing is as unrealistic as anonymity. Imagine a story whose hero has no name."

If your talk is full of names and personal pronouns you can be sure of high listenability, for you will have the priceless ingredient of human interest in your speech.

BE SPECIFIC, FILL YOUR TALK WITH DETAIL

You might say at this point, "this is all very fine, but how can I be sure of getting enough detail into my talk?" There is one test. Use the 5-W formula every reporter follows when he writes a news story: answer the questions When? Where? Who? What? and Why? If you follow this formula your examples will have life and color. Let me illustrate this with an anecdote of my own, one that was published by the *Reader's Digest:*

"After leaving college, I spent two years traveling through South Dakota as a salesman for Armour and Company. I covered my territory by riding on freight trains. One day I had to lay over in Redfield, S. D., for two hours to get a train going south. Since Redfield was not in my territory I couldn't use the time for making sales. Within a year I was going to New York to study at the American Academy of Dramatic Arts, so I decided to use this spare time practicing speaking. I wandered down through the train yards and began rehearsing a scene for *Macbeth*. Thrusting out my arms, I cried dramatically: 'Is this a dagger which I see before me, the handle toward my hand? Come, let me clutch thee: I have thee not, and yet I see thee still.'

"I was still immersed in the scene when four policemen leaped upon me and asked why I was frightening women. I couldn't have been more astounded if they had accused me of robbing a train. They informed me that a housewife had been watching me from behind her kitchen curtains a hundred yards away. She had never seen such goings-on. So she called the police, and when they approached they heard me ranting about daggers.

"I told them I was 'practicing Shakespeare,' but I had to produce my order book for Armour and Company before they let me go."

Notice how this anecdote answers the questions posed in the 5-W formula above.

Of course, too much detail is worse than none. All of us have been bored by lengthy recitals of superficial, irrelevant details. Notice how in the incident about my near-arrest in a South Dakota town there is a brief and concise answer to each of the 5-W questions. If you clutter your talk with too much detail, your audience will blue-pencil your remarks by refusing to give you their complete attention. There is no blue pencil more severe than inattentiveness.

DRAMATIZE YOUR TALK BY USING DIALOGUE

Suppose you want to give an illustration of how you succeeded in calming down an irate customer by using one of the rules of human relations. You could begin like this:

"The other day a man came into my office. He was pretty mad because the appliance we'had sent out to his house only the week before was not working properly. I told him that we would do all we could to remedy the situation. After a while he calmed down and seemed satisfied that we had every intention to make things right." This anecdote has one virtue—it is fairly specific—but it lacks names, specific details, and, above all, the actual dialogue which would make this incident come alive. Here it is with these added qualities:

"Last Tuesday, the door of my office slammed and I looked up to see the angry features of Charles Blexam, one of my regular customers. I didn't have time to ask him to take a seat. 'Ed, this is the last straw,' he said, 'you can send a truck right out and cart that wash machine out of my basement.'

"I asked him what was up. He was too willing to reply.

" 'It won't work,' he shouted, the clothes get all tangled, and my wife's sick and tired of it.'

"I asked him to sit down and explain it in more detail.

" 'haven't got time to sit down. I'm late for work and I wish I'd never come in here to buy an appliance in the first place. Believe me, I'll never do it again.' Here he hit the desk with his hand and knocked over my wife's picture.

" 'Look, Charley,' I said, 'if you will just sit down and tell me all about it, I promise to do whatever you want me to do.' With that, he sat down, and we calmly talked it over."

It isn't always possible to work dialogue into your talk, but you can see how the direct quotation of the conversation in the excerpt above helps to dramatize the incident for the listener. If the speaker has some imitative skill and can get the original tone of voice into the words, dialogue can become more effective. Also, dialogue gives your speech the authentic ring of everyday conversation. It makes you sound like a real person talking across a dinner table, not like a pedant delivering a paper before a learned society or an orator ranting into a microphone.

VISUALIZE BY DEMONSTRATING WHAT YOU ARE TALKING ABOUT

Psychologists tell us that more than eighty-five per cent of our knowledge comes to us through visual impressions. No doubt this accounts for the enormous effectiveness of television as an advertising as well as entertainment medium. Public speaking, too, is a visual as well as auditory art.

One of the best ways to enrich a talk with detail is to incorporate visual demonstration into it. You might spend hours just telling me how to swing a golf club, and I might be bored by it. But get up and show me what you do when you drive a ball down the fairway and I am all eyes and ears. Likewise, if you describe the erratic maneuvers of an airplane with your arms and shoulders, I am more intent on the outcome of your brush with death.

I remember a talk given in an industrial class that was a masterpiece of visual detail. The speaker was poking good-natured fun at inspectors and efficiency experts. His mimicry of the gestures and bodily antics of these gentlemen as they inspected a broken-down machine was more hilarious than anything I have ever seen on television. What is more, visual detail made that talk memorable—I for one shall never forget it, and I am sure the other members of that class are still talking about it.

It is a good idea to ask yourself, "How can I put some visual detail into my talk?" Then proceed to demonstrate, for, as the ancient Chinese observed, one picture is worth ten thousand words.

FOURTH

Use Concrete, Familiar Words that Create Pictures

In the process of getting and holding attention, which is

the first purpose of every speaker, there is one aid, one technique, that is of the highest importance. Yet, it is all but ignored. The average speaker does not seem to be aware of its existence. He has probably never consciously thought about it at all. I refer to the process of using words that create pictures. The speaker who is easy to listen to is the one who sets images floating before your eyes. The one who employs foggy, commonplace, colorless symbols sets the audience to nodding.

Pictures, Pictures. Pictures. They are as free as the air you breathe. Sprinkle them through your talks, your conversation, and you will be more entertaining, more influential.

Herbert Spencer, in his famous essay on the "Philosophy of Style," pointed out long ago the superiority of terms that call forth bright pictures:

"We do not think in generals but in particulars.... We should avoid such a sentence as:

"In proportion as the manners, customs, and amusements of a nation are cruel and barbarous, the regulations of their penal code will be severe!'

"And in place of it, we should write:

" 'In proportion as men delight in battles, bull fights, and combats of gladiators, will they punish by hanging, burning, and the rack.'

Picture-building phrases swarm through the pages of the Bible and through Shakespeare like bees around a cider mill. For example, a commonplace writer would have said that a certain thing would be "superfluous," like trying to improve the perfect. How did Shakespeare express the same thought? With a picture phrase that is immortal: "To gild refined gold, to paint the lily, to throw perfume on the violet."

Did you ever pause to observe that the proverbs that are passed on from generation to generation are almost all visual sayings? "A bird in the hand is worth two in the bush." "It never rains but it pours." "You can lead a horse to water but you can't make him drink." And you will find the same picture element in almost all the similes that have lived for centuries and grown hoary with too much use: "Sly as a fox." "Dead as a doornail." "Flat as a pancake." "Hard as a rock."

Lincoln continually talked in visual terminology. When he became annoyed with the long, complicated, red-tape reports that came to his desk in the White House, he objected to them, not with colorless phraseology, but with a picture phrase that it is almost impossible to forget. "When I send a man to buy a horse," he said, "I don't want to be told how many hairs the horse has in his tail. I wish only to know his points."

Make your eye appeals definite and specific. Paint mental pictures that stand out as sharp and clear as a stag's antlers silhouetted against the setting sun. For example, the word "dog" calls up a more or less definite picture of such an animal—perhaps a cocker spaniel, a Scottish terrier, a St. Bernard, or a Pomeranian. Notice how much more distinct an image springs into your mind when a speaker says "bulldog"—the term is less inclusive. Doesn't "a brindle bulldog" call up a still more explicit picture? Is it not more vivid to say "a black Shetland pony" than to talk of "a horse"? Doesn't "a white bantam rooster with a broken leg" give a much more definite and sharp picture than merely the word "fowl"?

In *The Elements of Style,* William Strunk, Jr., states: "If those who have studied the art of writing are in accord on any one point, it is on this: the surest way to arouse and hold the attention of the reader is by being specific, definite, and concrete. The greatest writers—Homer, Dante,

Shakespeare—are effective largely because they deal in particulars and report the details that matter. Their words call up pictures." This is as true of speaking as of writing.

I once devoted a session years ago in my course in Effective Speaking to an experiment in being factual. We adopted a rule that in every sentence the speaker must put either a fact or a proper noun, a figure, or a date. The results were revolutionary. The class members made a game of catching one another on generalities; it wasn't long before they were talking, not the cloudy language that floats over the head of an audience, but the clear-cut, vigorous language of the man on the street.

"An abstract style," said the French philosopher Alain," is always bad. Your sentences should be full of stones, metals, chairs, tables, animals, men, and women."

This is true of everyday conversation as well. In fact, all that has been said in this chapter about the use of detail in talks before groups applies to general conversation. It is detail that makes conversation sparkle. Anyone who is intent upon making himself a more effective conversationalist may profit by following the advice contained in this chapter. Salesmen, too, will discover the magic of detail when applied to their sales presentations. Those in executive positions, housewives, and teachers will find that giving instructions and dispensing information will be greatly improved by the use of concrete, factual detail.

If you can't write your message in a sentence, you can't say it in an hour.

—Dianna Booher

Tell the audience what you're going to say, say it; then tell them what you've said.

—Dale Carnegie

Chapter 8

VITALIZING THE TALK

Right after the First World War, I was in London working with Lowell Thomas, who was giving a series of brilliant lectures on Allenby and Lawrence of Arabia to packed houses. One Sunday I wandered into Hyde Park to the spot near Marble Arch entrance where speakers of every creed, color, and political and religious persuasion are allowed to air their views without interference from the law. For a while I listened to a Catholic explaining the doctrine of the infallibility of the Pope, then I moved to the fringes of another crowd, intent upon what a Socialist had to say about Karl Marx. I strolled over to a third speaker, who was explaining why it was right and proper for a man to have four wives! Then I moved away and looked back at the three groups.

Would you believe it? The man who was talking about polygamy had the fewest number of people listening to him! There was only a handful. The crowds around the other two speakers were growing larger by the minute. I asked myself why? Was it the disparity of topics? I don't think so. The explanation, I saw as I watched, was to be found in the speakers themselves. The fellow who was talking about the advantages of having fout wives didn't seem to be interested in having four wives himself. But the other two speakers, talking from almost diametrically opposed points of view, were wrapped up in their subjects. They talked with life and spirit. Their arms moved in impassioned gestures. Their voices rang with conviction. They radiated earnestness and animation.

Vitality, aliveness, enthusiasm—these are the first qualities I have always considered essential in a speaker. People cluster around the energetic speaker like wild turkeys around a field of autumn wheat.

How do you acquire this vital delivery that will keep the attention of your audience? In the course of this chapter I will give you three sovereign ways to help you put enthusiasm and excitement into your speaking.

FIRST

Choose Subjects You Are Earnest About

In Chapter Three was stressed the importance of feeling deeply about your subject. Unless you are emotionally involved in the subject matter you have chosen to talk about, you cannot expect to make your audience believe in your message. Obviously, if you select a topic that is exciting to you because of long experience with it, such as a hobby or recreational pursuit, or because of deep reflection or personal concern about it (as, for instance, the need for better schools in your community), you will have no difficulty in talking with excitement. The persuasive power of earnestness was never more vividly demonstrated to me than in a talk made before one of my classes in New York City more than two decades ago. I have heard many persuasive talks, but this one, which I call the Case of Blue Grass vs. Hickory Wood Ashes, stands out as a kind of triumph of sincerity over common sense.

A top-flight salesman of one of the best-known selling organizations in the city made the preposterous statement that he had been able to make blue grass grow without the aid of seeds or roots. He had, according to his story, scattered hickory wood ashes over newly plowed ground. Presto! Blue grass had appeared! He firmly believed that the hickory wood ashes, and the hickory wood ashes alone, were responsible for the blue grass.

Commenting on his talk, I gently pointed out to him that his phenomenal discovery would, if true, make him a millionaire, for blue grass seed was worth several dollars a bushel. I also told him that it would make him the outstanding scientist of all history. I informed him that no man, living or dead, had ever been able to perform the miracle he claimed to have performed: no man had ever been able to produce life from inert matter.

I told him that very quietly, for I felt that his mistake was so palpable, so absurd, as to require no emphasis in the refutation. When I had finished, every other member of the course saw the folly of his assertion; but he did not see it, not for a second. He was in earnest about his contention, deadly in earnest. He leaped to his feet and informed me that he was *not* wrong. He had not been relating theory, he protested, but personal experience. He *knew* whereof he spoke. He continued to talk, enlarging on his first remarks, giving additional information, piling up additional evidence, sincerity and honesty ringing in his voice.

Again I informed him that there was not the remotest hope in the world of his being right or even approximately right or within a thousand miles of the truth. In a second he was on his feet once more, offering to bet me five dollars and to let the U. S. Department of Agriculture settle the matter.

And do you know what happened? Several members in the class were won over to his side. Many others were beginning to be doubtful. If I had taken a vote I am certain that more than half of the businessmen in that class would not have sided with me. I asked them what had shaken them from their original position. One after another said it was the speaker's earnestness, his belief, so energetically stated, that made them begin to doubt the common sense viewpoint.

Well, in the face of that display of credulity I had to write the Department of Agriculture. I was ashamed, I told them, to ask such an absurd question. They replied, of course, that it was impossible to get blue grass or any other living thing frotn hickory wood ashes, and they added that they had received another letter from New York asking the same question. That salesman was so sure of his position that he sat down and wrote a letter, too!

This incident taught me a lesson I'll never forget. *lf a speaker believes a thing earnestly enough and says it earnestly enough, he will get adherents to his cause,* even though he claims he can produce blue grass from dust and ashes. How much more compelling will our convictions be if they are arrayed on the side of common sense and truth!

Almost all speakers wonder whether the topic they have chosen will interest the audience. There is only one way to make sure that they will be interested: stoke the fires of your enthusiasm for the subject and you will have no difficulty holding the interest of a group of people.

A short time ago, I heard a man in one of our classes in Baltimore warn his audience that if the present methods of catching rock fish in Chesapeake Bay were continued the species would become extinct. And in a very few years! He felt his subject. It was important. He was in real earnest about it. Everything about his matter and manner showed that. When he arose to speak, I did not know that there was such a creature as a rock fish in Chesapeake Bay. I imagine that more of the audience shared my lack of knowledge and lack of interest. But before the speaker finished, all of us would probably have been willing to sign a petition to the legislature to protect the rock fish by law.

Richard Washburn Child, the former American Ambassador to Italy, was once asked the secret of his success as an interesting writer. He replied: "I am so excited about life that I cannot keep still. I just have to tell people about it." One cannot keep from being enthralled with a speaker or writer like that.

I once went to hear a speaker in London; after he was through, one of our party, Mr. E. F. Benson, a well-known English novelist, remarked that he enjoyed the last part of the talk far more than the first. When I asked him why, he replied: "The speaker himself seemed more interested in the last part, and I always rely on the speaker to supply the enthusiasm and interest."

Here is another illustration of the importance of choosing your topics well.

A gentleman, whom we shall call Mr. Flynn, was enrolled in one of our classes in Washington, D. C. One evening early in the course, he devoted his talk to a description of the capital city of the United States. He had hastily and superficially gleaned his facts from a booklet issued by a local newspaper. They sounded like it—dry, disconnected, undigested. Though he had lived in Washington for many years, he did not present one personal instance of why he liked the city. He merely recited a series of dull facts, and his talk was as distressing for the class to hear as it was agonizing for him to give.

A fortnight later, something happened that touched Mr. Flynn to the core: an unknown driver had smashed into his new car while it was parked on the street and had driven away without identifying himself. It was impossible for Mr. Flynn to collect insurance and he had to foot the bill himself.

Here was something that came hot out of his experience. His talk about the city of Washington, which he laboriously pulled out sentence by sentence, was painful to him and his audience; but when he spoke about his smashed-up car, his talk welled up and boiled forth like Vesuvius in action. The same class that had squirmed restlessly in their seats two weeks before now greeted Mr. Flynn with a heart warming burst of applause.

As I have pointed out repeatedly, you cannot help but succeed if you choose the right topic for you. One area of topics is sure-fire: talk about your convictions! Surely you have strong beliefs about some aspect of life around you. You don't have to search far and wide for these subjects—they generally lie on the surface of your stream of consciousness, because you often think about them.

Not long ago, a legislative hearing on capital punishment was presented on television. Many witnesses were called to give their viewpoints on both sides of this controversial subject. One of them was a member of the police department of the city of Los Angeles, who had evidently given much thought to this topic. He had strong convictions based on the fact that eleven of his fellow police officers had been killed in gun battles with criminals. He spoke with the deep sincerity of one who believed to his heart's core in the righteousness of his cause. The greatest appeals in the history of eloquence have all been made out of the depths of someone's deep convictions and feelings. Sincerity rests upon belief, and belief is as much a matter of the heart and of warmly feeling what you are saying as it is of the mind and coldly thinking of what to say. "The heart has reasons that the reason does not know." In many classes I have had frequent occasions to verify Pascal's trenchant sentence. I remember a lawyer in Boston who was blessed with a striking appearance and who spoke with admirable fluency, but when he finished speaking people said: "Clever chap." He made a surface impression because there never seemed to be any feeling behind his glittering facade of words. In the same class, there was an insurance salesman, small in stature, unprepossessing in appearance, a man who groped for a word now and then, but when he spoke there was no doubt in any of his listeners' minds that he felt every word of his talk. It is almost a hundred years since Abraham Lincoln's assassination in the presidential box of Ford's Theatre in Washington, D. C., but the deep sincerity of his life and his words still lives with us. As far as knowledge of law is concerned, scores of other men of his time outstripped him. He lacked grace, smoothness, and polish. But the honesty and sincerity of his utterances at Gettysburg, Cooper Union, and on the steps of the Capitol in Washington, have not been surpassed in our history.

You may say, as one man once did, that you have no strong convictions or interests. I am always a little surprised at this, but I told this man to get busy and get interested in something. "What, for instance?" he asked. In desperation I said, "Pigeons." "Pigeons?" he asked in a bewildered tone. "Yes," I told him, "pigeons. Go out on the square and look at them, feed them, go to the library and read about them, then come back here and talk about them." He did. When he came back there was no holding him down. He started to talk about pigeons with all the fervor of a fancier. When I tried to stop him he was saying something about forty books on pigeons and he had read them all. He gave one of the most interesting talks I have ever heard.

Here is another suggestion: Learn more and more about what you now consider a pretty good topic. The more you know about something the more earnest and excitedly enthusiastic you will become. Percy H. Whiting, the author of the *Five Great Rules of Selling,* tells salesmen never to stop learning about the product they are selling. As Mr. Whiting says, "The more you know about a good product, the more enthusiastic you become about it." The same thing is true about your topics—the more you know about them, the more earnest and enthusiastic you will be about them.

SECOND

Relive the Feelings You Have About Your Topic

Suppose you are telling your audience about the policeman who stopped you for going one mile over the speed limit. You can tell us that with all the cool disinterestedness of an onlooker, but it happened to you and you had certain feelings which you expressed in quite definite language. The third-person approach will not make much of an impression on your audience. They want to know exactly how you felt when that policeman wrote out that ticket. So, the more you relive the scene you are describing, or recreate the emotions you felt originally, the more vividly you will express yourself.

One of the reasons why we go to plays and movies is that we want to hear and see emotions expressed. We have become so fearful of giving vent to our feelings in public that we have to go to a play to satisfy this need for emotional expression.

When you speak in public, therefore, you will generate excitement and interest in your talk in proportion to the amount of excitement you put into it. Don't repress your honest feelings; don't put a damper on your authentic enthusiasms. Show your listeners how eager you are to talk about your subject, and you will hold their attention.

THIRD

Act in Earnest

When you walk before your audience to speak, do so with an air of anticipation, not like a man who is ascending the gallows. The spring in your walk may be largely put on, but it will do wonders for you and it gives the audience the feeling that you have something you are eager to talk about. Just before you begin, take a deep breath. Keep away from furniture or from the speaker's stand. Keep your head high and your chin up. You are about to tell your listeners something worthwhile, and every part of you should inform them of that clearly and unmistakably. You are in command, and as William James would say, act as if you are. If you make an effort to send your voice to the back of the hall, the sound will reassure you. Once you begin making gestures of any kind, they will help to stimulate you.

This principle of "warming up our reactivity," as Donald and Eleanor Laird describe it, can be applied to all situations that demand mental awareness. In their book *Techniques for Efficient Remembering,* the Lairds point to President Theodore Roosevelt as a man who "breezed through life with a bounce, vigor, dash, and enthusiasm which became his trademark. He was absorbingly interested, or effectively pretended he was, in everything he tackled." Teddy Roosevelt was a living exponent of the philosophy of William James: "Act in earnest and you will become naturally earnest in all you do."

Above all, remember this: acting in earnest will make you feel earnest.

If you don't know what you want to achieve in your presentation your audience never will.

—Harvey Diamond

There are always three speeches, for every one you actually gave. The one you practiced, the one you gave, and the one you wish you gave.

—Dale Carnegie

Chapter 9

DELIVERING THE TALK

Would you believe it? There are four ways, and only four ways, in which we have contact with the world. We are evaluated and classified by these four contacts: what we do, how we look, what we say, and how we say it. This chapter will deal with the last of these—how we say it.

When I first started to teach public speaking classes, I spent a great deal of time on the use of vocal exercises to develop resonance, increase the range of voice, and enhance inflectional agility. It wasn't long, however, before I began to see the utter futility of teaching adults how to project their tones into the upper sinuses and how to form "liquid" vowels. This is all very fine for those who can devote three or four years to improving themselves in the art of vocal delivery. I realized that my students would have to settle for the vocal equipment they were born with. I found that if I expended the time and energy I formerly devoted to helping class members to "breathe diaphragmatcally-" and workcd on the far more important objectives of freeing them from their inhibitions and general reluctance to let themselves go, I would achieve quick and lasting results that were truly amazing. I thank God I had the sense to do this.

FIRST

Crash Through Your Shell of Self-Consciousness

In my course there are several sessions that have as their purpose the freeing of tightly bound and tense adults. I got down on my knees, literally, to implore my class members to come out of their shells and find out for themselves that the world would treat them with cordiality and welcome when they would do so. It took some doing, I admit, but it was worth it. As Marshal Foch says of the art of war, "it is simple enough in its conception, but unfortunately complicated in its execution." The biggest stumbling block, of course, is stiffness, not only of the physical, but of the mental as well, a kind of hardening of the categories that comes with growing up.

It is not easy to be natural before an audience. Actors know that. When you were a child, say, four years old, you probably could have mounted a platform and talked naturally to an audience. But when you are twenty-and-four, or forty-and-four, what happens when you mount a platform and start to speak? Do you retain that unconscious naturalness that you possessed at four? You may, but it is dollars to doughnuts that you will become stiff and stilted and mechanical, and draw back into your shell like a snapping turtle.

The problem of teaching or of training adults in delivery is not one of superimposing additional characteristics; it is largely one of removing impediments, of getting them to speak with the same naturalness that they would display if someone were to knock them down.

Hundreds of times I have stopped speakers in the midst of their talks and implored them to "talk like a human being." Hundreds of nights I have come home mentally fatigued and nervously exhausted from trying to drill members of my classes to talk naturally. No, believe me, it is not so easy as it sounds.

In one of the sessions of my course I ask the class to act out portions of dialogue, some of which is in dialect. I ask them to throw themselves into these dramatic episodes with abandon. When they do, they discover to their amazement that, though they may have acted like a fool, they didn't feel badly when they were doing it. The class too is amazed at the dramatic ability some of the class members display. My point is that once you let your hair down before a group you are not likely to hold yourself back when it comes to the normal, everyday expression of your opinions whether to individuals or before groups.

The sudden freedom you feel is like a bird taking wing after being imprisoned in a cage. You see why it is that people flock to the theater and the movies—because there they see their fellow human beings act with little or no inhibition, there they see people wearing their emotions prominently displayed on their sleeves.

SECOND

Don't Try to Imitate Others—Be Yourself

We all admire speakers who can put showmanship into their speaking, who are not afraid to express themselves, not afraid to use the unique, individual, imaginative way of saying what they have to say to the audience.

Shortly after the close of the First World War, I met two brothers in London, Sir Ross and Sir Keith Smith. They had just made the first aeroplane flight from London to Australia to win a fifty-thousand-dollar prize offered by the Australian government. They had created a sensation throughout the British Empire and had been knighted by the King.

Captain Hurley, a well-known scenic photographer, had flown with them over a part of their trip, taking motion pictures; so I helped them prepare an illustrated travel talk of their flight and trained them in the delivery of it. They gave it twice daily for four months in Philharmonic Hall, London, one speaking in the afternoon, the other at night.

They had had identically the same experience, they had sat side by side as they flew halfway around the world, and they delivered the same talk, almost word for word. Yet, somehow it didn't sound like the same talk at all.

There is something besides the mere words in a talk which counts. It is the flavor with which they are delivered. It is not so much just what you say as how you say it.

Brulloff, the great Russian painter, once corrected a pupil's study. The pupil looked in amazement at the altered drawing, exclaiming: "Why, you have touched it only a tiny bit, but it is quite another thing." Brulloff replied, "Art begins where the tiny bit begins." That is as true of speaking as it is of painting and of Paderewski's playing.

The same thing holds true when one is touching words. There is an old saying in the English Parliament that everything depends upon the manner in which one speaks and not upon the matter. Quintilian said it long ago, when England was one of the outlying colonies of Rome.

"All Fords are exactly alike," their maker used to say, but no two men are just alike. Every new life is a new thing under the sun; there has never been anything just like it before, and never will be again. A young man ought to get that idea about himself; he should look for the single spark of individuality that makes him different from other folks, and develop that for all he is worth. Society and schools may try to iron it out of him; their tendency is to put us all in the same mold but, I say, don't let that spark be lost; it's your only real claim to importance.

All that is doubly true of effective speaking. There is no other human being in the world like you. Hundreds of millions of people have two eyes and a nose and a mouth; but none of them looks precisely like you; and none of them has exactly your traits and methods and cast of mind. Few of them will talk and express themselves just as you do when you are speaking naturally. In other words, you have an individuality. As a speaker, it is your most precious possession. Cling to it. Cherish it. Develop it. It is the spark that will put force and sincerity into your speaking. "It is your only real claim to importance." Please, I beg you, do not attempt to force yourself in a mold and thereby lose your distinctiveness.

THIRD

Converse with Your Audience

Let me give you an illustration that is typical of the fashion in which thousands of persons talk. I happened on one occasion to be stopping in Murren, a summer resort in the Swiss Alps. I was living at a hotel operated by a London company; and they usually sent out from England a couple of lecturers each week to talk to the guests. One of them was a well-known English novelist. Her topic was "The Future of the Novel." She admitted that she had not selected the subject herself; and the long and short of it was that she had nothing she cared to say about it to make it worthwhile expressing. She had hurriedly made some rambling notes; and she stood before the audience, ignoring her hearers, not even looking at them, staring sometimes over their heads, sometimes at her notes, sometimes at the floor. She unreeled words into the primeval void with a far-away look in her eyes and a far-away ring in her voice.

That isn't delivering a talk at all. It is a soliloquy. It has no *sense of communication.* And that is the first essential of good talking: a *sense of communication*. The audience must feel that there is a message being delivered straight from the mind and heart of the speaker to their minds and their hearts. The kind of talk I have just described might as well have been spoken out in the sandy, waterless wastes of the Gobi desert. In fact, it sounded as if it were being delivered in some such spot rather than to a group of living human beings.

An enormous amount of nonsense and twaddle has been written about delivery. It has been shrouded in rules and rites and made mysterious. Old-fashioned "elocution" has often made it ridiculous. The businessman, going to the library or book shop, has found volumes on "oratory" that were utterly useless. In spite of progress in other directions, in almost every state in the Union today, schoolboys are still being forced to recite the ornate "oratory of 'orators' "—a thing that is as useless as a squirrel-headed tire pump, as out-of-date as a quill pen.

An entirely new school of speaking has sprung up since the twenties. In keeping with the spirit of the times, it is as modern and as practical as the automobile, direct as a telegram, businesslike as a telling advertisement. The verbal fireworks that were once the vogue would no longer be tolerated by an audience today.

A modern audience, regardless of whether it is fifteen people at a business conference or a thousand people under a tent, wants the speaker to talk just as directly as he would in a chat, and in the same general manner he would employ in speaking to one of them in conversation, in the same *manner,* but with greater force or energy. In order to appear natural, he has to use much more energy in talking to forty people than he does in talking to one, just as a statue on top of a building has to be of heroic size in order to make it appear of lifelike proportions to an observer on the ground.

At the close of one of Mark Twain's lectures in a Nevada mining camp, an old prospector approached him and inquired: "Be them your natural tones of eloquence?"

That is what the audience wants: "your natural tones of eloquence," enlarged a bit. The only way to acquire the knack of this enlarged naturalness is by practice. And, as you practice, if you find yourself talking in a stilted manner, pause and say sharply to yourself mentally: "Here! What is wrong? Wake up! Be human." Then mentally pick out a person in the audience, someone in the back or the least attentive person you can find, and talk to this person. Forget there is anyone else present at all. *Converse* with this person. Imagine that he has asked you a question and that you are answering it, and that you are the *only* one who can answer it. If he were to stand up and talk to you, and you were to talk back to him, that process would immediately and inevitably make your speaking more conversational, more natural, more direct. So, imagine that is precisely what is taking place.

You may go so far as actually to ask questions and answer them. For example, in the midst of your talk, you may say, "and you ask what proof have I for this assertion? I have adequate proof and here it is..." Then proceed to answer the question. That sort of thing can be done very naturally. It will break up the monotony of one's delivery; it will make it direct and pleasant and conversational.

Speak to the Chamber of Commerce just as you would to John Henry Smith. What is a meeting of the Chamber of Commerce, after all, but a collection of John Henry Smiths? Won't the same methods that are successful with those men individually be successful with them collectively?

Earlier in this chapter was described the delivery of a certain novelist. In the same ballroom in which she had spoken, we had the pleasure, a few nights later, of hearing Sir

Oliver Lodge. His subject was "Atoms and Worlds." He had devoted to this subject more than half a century of thought and study and experiment and investigation. He had something that was essentially a part of his heart and mind and life, something that he wanted very much to say. He forgot that he was trying to make a "speech." That was the least of his worries. He was concerned only with telling the audience about atoms, telling us accurately, lucidly, and feelingly. He was earnestly trying to get us to see what he saw and to feel what he felt.

And what was the result? He delivered a remarkable talk. It had both charm and power. It made a deep impression. He was a speaker of unusual ability. Yet I am sure he didn't regard himself in that light. I am sure that few people who heard him ever thought of him as a "public speaker" at all.

If you speak in public so that people hearing you will suspect that you have had training in public speaking, you will not be a credit to your instructor, especially an instructor in one of my courses. He desires you to speak with such intensified naturalness that your audience will never dream that you have been "formally" trained. A good window does not call attention to itself. It merely lets in the light. A good speaker is like that. He is so disarmingly natural that his hearers never notice his manner of speaking: they are conscious only of his matter.

FOURTH

Put Your Heart into Your Speaking

Sincerity and enthusiasm and high earnestness will help you, too. When a man is under the influence of his feelings, his real self comes to the surface. The bars are down. The heat of his emotions has burned all barriers away. He acts spontaneously. He talks spontaneously. He is natural.

So, in the end, even this matter of delivery comes back to

the thing which has already been emphasized repeatedly in these pages: namely, *put your heart into your talks.*

"I shall never forget," said Dean Brown in his Lectures on Preaching before the Yale Divinity School, "the description given by a friend of mine of a church service which he once attended in the city of London. The preacher was George MacDonald; he read for the Scripture lesson that morning the eleventh chapter of Hebrews. When the time came for the sermon, he said: `You have all heard about these men of faith. I shall not try to tell you what faith is. There are theological professors who could do that much better than I could do it. I am here to help you believe.' Then followed such a simple, heartfelt, and majestic manifestation of the man's own faith in those unseen realities which are eternal, as to beget faith in the minds and hearts of all his hearers. *His heart was in his work, and his delivery was effective because it rested upon the genuine beauty of his own inner life."*

"His heart was in his work." That is the secret. Yet I know that advice like this is not popular. It seems vague. It sounds indefinite. The average person wants foolproof rules, something definite, something he can put his hands on, rules as precise as the directions for operating a car.

That is what he wants; that is what I would like to give him. It would be easy for him and it would be easy for me. There are such rules, and there is only one little thing wrong with them: they just don't work. They take all the naturalness and spontaneity and life and juice out of a man's speaking. I know. In my younger days, I wasted a great deal of energy trying them. They won't appear in these pages for, as Josh Billings observed in one of his lighter moments: "There ain't no use in knowin' so many things that ain't so."

Edmund Burke wrote speeches so superb in logic and reasoning and composition that they are today studied as classic models of oratory in the colleges of the land; yet Burke, as a speaker, was a notorious failure. He didn't have the ability to deliver his gems, to make them interesting and forceful; so he was called "the dinner bell" of the House of Commons. When he arose to talk, the other members coughed and shuffled and either went to sleep or went out in droves.

You can throw a steel-jacketed bullet at a man with all your might, and you cannot make even a dent in his clothing. But put powder behind a tallow candle and you can shoot it through a pine board. Many a tallowcandle speech with powder makes, I regret to say, more of an impression than a steel-jacketed talk with no force, no excitement, behind it.

FIFTH

Practice Making Your Voice Strong and Flexible

When we are really communicating our ideas to our listeners we are making use of many elements of vocal and physical variety. We shrug our shoulders, move our arms, wrinkle our brows, increase our volume, change pitch and inflection, and talk fast or slow as the occasion and the material may dictate. It is well to remember that all these are effects and not causes. The so-called variables, or modulations of tone, are under the direct influence of our mental and emotional state. That is why it is so important that we have a topic we know and a topic we are excited about when we go before an audience. That is why we must be so eager to share that topic with our listeners. Since most of us lose the spontaneity and naturalness of youth as we grow older, we tend to slip into a definite mold of physical and vocal communication. We find ourselves less ready to use gestures and animation; we rarely raise or lower our voices from one pitch to another. In short, we lose the freshness and spontaneity of true conversation. We may get into the habit of talking too slowly or too rapidly, and our diction, unless carefully watched, tends to become ragged and careless. In this book you have been repeatedly told to act natural, and you may suppose that I therefore condone poor diction or monotonous delivery provided it is natural. On the contrary, I say that we should be natural in the sense that we express *our ideas* and express them with spirit. On the other hand, every good speaker will not accept himself as incapable of improvement in breadth of vocabulary, richness of imagery and diction, and variety and force of expression. These are areas in which everyone interested in self-improvement will seek to improve.

It is an excellent idea to evaluate oneself in terms of volume, pitch variation, and pace. This can be done with the aid of a tape recorder. On the other hand, it would be useful to have friends help you make this evaluation. If it is possible to secure expert advice, so much the better. It should be remembered, however, that these are areas for practice away from the audience. To concern yourself with technique when you are before an audience will prove fatal to effectiveness. Once there, pour yourself into your talk, concentrate your whole being on making a mental and emotional impact on your audience, and nine chances out of ten you will speak with more emphasis and force than you could ever get from books.

Best way to conquer stage fright is to know what you're talking about.

—Michael H. Mescon

There are four ways, and only four ways, in which we have contact with the world. We are evaluated and classified by these four contacts: what we do, how we look, what we say, and how we say it.

—Dale Carnegie

Chapter 10

SHARING THE TALK WITH THE AUDIENCE

Russell Conwell's famous lecture, "Acres of Diamonds," was given nearly six thousand times. You would think that a talk repeated so often would become set in the speaker's mind, that no word or intonation would vary in delivery. That was not the case. Dr. Conwell knew that audiences differ. He recognized that he had to make each successive audience feel that his talk was a personal, living thing created for it, and it alone. How did he succeed in keeping this interrelationship between speaker, speech, and audience alive from one speaking engagement to the next? "I visit a town or city," he wrote, "and try to arrive there early enough to see the postmaster, the barber, the hotel manager, the principal of the schools, some of the ministers, and then go into the stores and talk with people, and see what has been their history and what opportunities they had. Then I give my lecture and talk to those people about the subjects that apply to them locally."

Dr. Conwell was thoroughly aware that successful communication depends upon how well the speaker can make his talk a part of the listeners and the listeners a part of the talk. That is why we have no true copy of "Acres of Diamonds," one of the most popular talks ever given from a lecture platform. With his clever insight into human nature and his painstaking industry, Dr. Conwell did not give the same lecture twice, although he addressed almost six thousand different audiences on the same subject. You can profit from his example by making certain that your talks are always prepared with a specific audience in mind. Here are some simple rules that will help you to build up a strong feeling of rapport with your listeners.

FIRST

Talk in Terms of Your Listeners' Interests

That is exactly what Dr. Conwell did. He made a point of working into his lecture plenty of local allusions and examples. His audiences were interested because his talk concerned them, their interests, their problems. This linkage with what your hearers are most interested in, namely, themselves, will insure attention and guarantee that the lines of communication will remain open. Eric Johnston, former head of the United States Chamber of Commerce and now president of the Motion Picture Association, uses this technique in almost every talk he gives. Note how resourcefully he employed local interests in a commencement address at the University of Oklahoma:

You Oklahomans are well acquainted with goose-pimple peddlers. You don't have to think back too far to remember when they were writing Oklahoma off the books as a hopeless risk forever.

Why, in the 1930s, all the ravens of despair were telling the crows to bypass Oklahoma unless they could pack along their own rations.

They consigned Oklahoma to an everlasting future as part of a new American desert. Nothing would ever bloom again—they said. But in the 1940's Oklahoma was a garden spot—and the toast of Broadway. For, once again, there was "waving wheat that sure smells sweet when the wind comes right behind the rain."

In one short decade, the dustbowl was smothered with corn stalks as high as the elephant's eye.

Here was a pay-off for faith—and calculated risk...

But it is always possible to see our own times in better perspective against the backdrop of yesterday.

So I looked up the files of the *Daily Oklahoman* for the spring of 1901 in preparation for my visit here. I wanted to sample the flavor of life in the tetritory fifty years ago.

And what did I discover?

Why I found the big accent was all on Oklahoma's future. The big stress was on hope.

Here is an excellent example of talking in terms of audience interest. Eric Johnston used instances of calculated risk right out of his listeners' back yards. He made them feel that his talk was no mimeographed copy—it was freshly created for them. No audience can withhold attention from a speaker who talks in its interests.

Ask yourself how knowledge of your subject will help the members of your audience solve their problems and achieve their goals. Then proceed to show them that, and you will have their complete attention. If you are an accountant and you start your talk by saying something like this, "I am going to show you how to save from fifty to a hundred dollars on your tax return," or you are a lawyer and you tell your listeners how to go about making a will, you will be certain to have an interested audience. Surely, there is some topic in your special fund of knowledge that can be of real help to members of your audience.

When asked what interests people, Lord Northcliffe, the William Randolph Hearst of British journalism, replied, "themselves." He built a newspaper empire on that single truth.

In *Mind in the Making,* James Harvey Robinson describes reverie as "a spontaneous and favorite kind of thinking." He goes on to say that, in reverie, we allow our ideas to take their own course, and this course is determined by our hopes and fears, our spontaneous desires, their fulfillment or frustration; by our likes and dislikes, our loves, hates, and resentments. There is nothing so interesting to ourselves as ourselves.

Harold Dwight, of Philadelphia, made an extraordinarily successful talk at a banquet which marked the final session of our course. He talked about each person in turn around the entire table, how he had spoken when the course started, how he had improved; he recalled the talks various members had made, the subjects they had discussed; he mimicked some of them, exaggerated their peculiarities, had everyone laughing, had everyone pleased. With such material, he could not possibly have failed. It was absolutely ideal. No other topic under the blue dome of heaven would have so interested that group. Mr. Dwight knew how to handle human nature.

Some years ago I wrote a series of articles for the *American Magazine,* and I had the opportunity of talking with John Siddall, who was then in charge of the Interesting People Department.

"People are selfish," he said. "They are interested chiefly in themselves. They are not very much concerned about whether the government should own the railroads; but they do want to know how to get ahead, how to draw more salary, how to keep healthy. If I were editor of this magazine," he went on, "I would tell them how to take care of their teeth, how to take baths, how to keep cool in summer, how to get a position, how to handle employees, how to buy homes, how to remember, how to avoid grammatical error, and so on. People are always interested in human interest stories, so I would have some rich man tell how he made a million in real estate. I would get prominent bankers and presidents of various corporations to tell the stories of how they battled their ways up from the ranks to power and wealth."

Shortly after that, Siddall was made editor. The magazine then had a small circulation. Siddall did just what he said he would do. The response? It was overwhelming. The circulation figures climbed up to two hundred thousand, three, four, half a million. Here was something the public wanted. Soon a million people a month were buying it, then a million and a half, finally two million. It did not stop there, but continued to grow for many years. Siddall appealed to the self-interests of his readers.

The next time you face an audience, visualize them as eager to hear what you have to say—as long as it applies to them. Speakers who fail to take this essential egocentricity of their listeners into account are apt to find themselves facing a restless audience, one squirming in boredom, glancing at wristwatches, and looking hopefully toward the exit doors.

SECOND

Give Honest, Sincere Appreciation

Audiences are composed of individuals, and they react like individuals. Openly criticize an audience and they resent it. Show your appreciation for something they have done that is worthy of praise, and you win a passport into their hearts. This often requires some research on your part. Such fulsome phrases as "this is the most intelligent audience I have ever addressed," are resented as hollow flattery by most audiences.

In the words of a great speaker, Chauncey M. Depew, you have to "tell them something about themselves that they didn't think you could possibly know." For example, a man who spoke before the Baltimore Kiwanis Club recently could find nothing unusual about that club except that it had in its membership a past international president and an international trustee. This was no news to the members of the club. So he tried to give it a new twist. He started his talk with this sentence: "The Baltimore Kiwanis Club is one club in 101,898!" The members listened. This speaker was certainly wrong-because there were only 2,897 Kiwanis Clubs in the world. The speaker then went on:

Yes, even if you don't believe it, it is still a fact that your club, mathematically at least, is one in 101,898. Not one club in 100,000 or one in 200,000, but just exactly one in 101,898.

How do I figure that out? Kiwanis International has only 2,897 member clubs. Well, the Baltimore club has a past president of Kiwanis International and an international trustee. Mathematically, the chances that any Kiwanis club will have both a past president and an international trustee at the same time are one in 101,898—and the reason I know it's right is that I got a Johns Hopkins Ph.D. in mathematics to figure it out for me.

Be exactly one hundred per cent sincere. An insincere statement may occasionally fool an individual, but it never fools an audience. "This highly intelligent audience..." "This exceptional gathering of the beauty and chivalry of HoHokus, New Jersey..." "I'm glad to be here because I love each one of you." No, no, no! If you can't show sincere appreciation, don't show any!

THIRD

Identify Yourself with the Audience

As soon as possible, preferably in the first words you utter, indicate some direct relationship with the group you are addressing. If you are honored by being asked to speak, say so. When Harold Macmillan spoke to the graduating class at De Pauw University in Greencastle, Indiana, he opened up the lines of communication in his first sentence.

"I am very grateful for your kind words of welcome," he said, "For a Prime Minister of Great Britain to be invited to your great university is an unusual occasion. But I feel that my present office was not the only nor, indeed, perhaps the main reason for your invitation."

Then he mentioned that his mother was an American, born in Indiana, and that her father had been one of De Pauw's first graduates.

"I can assure you that I am proud to be associated with De Pauw University," he said, "and to renew an old family tradition."

You may be sure that Macmillan's reference to an American school and to the American way of life which his mother and her pioneer father knew made friends for him at once.

Another way to open the lines of communication is to use the names of people in the audience. I once sat next to the main speaker at a banquet and I was amazed at his curiosity concerning various people in the hall. All through the meal he kept asking the master of ceremonies who the person in the blue suit at one table was, or what was the name of the lady in the flowered hat. When he arose to speak, it became evident at once why he was curious. He very cleverly wove some of the names he had learned into his talk, and I could see the evident pleasure on the faces of the persons whose names were used and I sensed the warm friendliness of the audience that this simple technique won for the speaker.

Notice how Frank Pace, Jr., speaking as the president of

the General Dynamics Corporation, worked in a few names to advantage. He was speaking at an annual dinner of Religion in American Life, Inc., in New York:

"This has been a delightful and meaningful evening for me in many ways," he said. "First, I have my own minister, the Reverend Robert Appleyard, here in the audience. By his words, deeds, and leadership he has been an inspiration to me personally, to my family, and to our entire congregation. Secondly, to sit between Lewis Strauss and Bob Stevens, men whose interest in religion has been amplified by their interest in public service...is again a source of great personal pleasure..."

One word of caution: If you are going to work strange names into your talk, having learned them through inquiries made for the occasion, be sure you have them exactly right; be sure you understand fully the reason for your use of the names; be sure you mention them only in a favorable way; and use them in moderation.

Another method of keeping the audience at peak attentiveness is to use the pronoun "you" rather than the third-person "they." In this way you keep the audience in a state of self-awareness, which I have pointed out earlier cannot be overlooked by the speaker if he is to hold the interest and attention of his listeners. Here are some excerpts from a talk on Sulphuric Acid by one of our students in a New York City class:

Sulphuric acid touches you in your life in a score of ways. If it were not for sulphuric acid, your car would stop, for it is used extensively in the refining of kerosene and gasoline. The electric lights that illuminate your office and your home would not be possible without it.

When you turn on the water for your bath, you use a nickel-plated faucet, which requires sulphuric acid in its manufacture. The soap you use has possibly been made from greases or oils that have been treated with the acid. The bristles in your hairbrush and your celluloid comb could not have been produced without it. Your razor, no doubt, has been pickled in it after annealing.

You come down to breakfast. The cup and saucer, if they are other than plain white, could not have come into being without it. Your spoon, knife and fork have seen a bath of sulphuric acid if they are silver-plated. And so on through the whole day sulphuric acid affects you at every turn. Go where you will, you cannot escape its influence.

By skillfully using "you" and inserting his listeners into the picture, this speaker was able to keep attention alive and glowing. There are times, however, when the pronoun "you" is dangerous, when it may establish a cleavage between speaker and audience rather than a bridge. This occurs when it might seem as though we were talking down to our audience or lecturing it. Then it is better to say "we" instead of "you."

Dr. W. W. Bauer, Director of Health Education of the American Medical Association, often used this technique in his radio and television talks. "We all want to know how to choose a good doctor, don't we?" he said in one of his talks. "And if we are going to get the best service from our doctor, don't we all want to know how to be good patients?"

FOURTH

Make Your Audience a Partner in Your Talk

Did it ever occur to you that you can keep an audience hanging on every word by using a little showmanship? The moment you choose some member of the audience to help you demonstrate a point or dramatize an idea, you will be rewarded by a noticeable rise in attention. Being aware of themselves as an audience, the members of it are keenly conscious of what happens when one of its own is brought into "the act" by the speaker. If there is a wall between the man on the platform and the people out there, as many speakers say, the use of audience participation will break that wall down. I remember a speaker who was explaining the distance it takes to stop a car after the brakes have been applied. He asked one of his listeners in the front row to stand and help demonstrate how this distance varied with the speed of the car. The man in the audience took the end of a steel tape measure and carried it forty-five feet down the aisle, where he stopped on a signal from the speaker. As I watched this procedure I couldn't help but notice how the whole audience became engrossed in the talk. I said to myself that the tape measure, in addition to being a graphic illustration of the speaker's point, was certainly a line of communication between that speaker and this audience. Without that touch of showmanship the audience might still be concerned with what it was going to have for dinner or what programs would be on TV that evening.

One of my favorite methods of getting audience participation is simply to ask questions and to get responses, I like to get the audience on its feet, repeating a sentence after me, or answering my questions by raising their hands. Percy H. Whiting, whose book *How to Put Humor in Your Speaking and Writing* contains some valuable advice on the subject of audience participation, suggests having your listeners vote on something, or inviting them to help you solve a problem. "Get yourself in the right state of mind," says Mr. Whiting, "a state of mind that recognizes that a speech is unlike a recitation–that it is designed to get audience reaction–to make the audience a partner in the enterprise." I like that description of the audience as "a partner in the enterprise." It is the key to what this chapter is all about. If you use audience participation you confer the rights of partnership on your listeners.

FIFTH

Ploy Yourself Down

Of course, nothing will take the place of sincerity in this speaker-audience relationship. Norman Vincent Peale once gave some very useful advice to a fellow minister who was having great difficulty keeping the audience intent upon his sermons. He asked this minister to question his feelings about the congregation he addressed each Sunday morning—did he like them, did he want to help them, did he consider them his intellectual inferiors? Dr. Peale said that he never ascended the pulpit without feeling a strong sense of affection for the men and women he was about to face. An audience is quick in taking the measure of a speaker who assumes that he is superior in mental accomplishment or in social standing. Indeed, one of the best ways for a speaker to endear himself to an audience is to play himself down.

Edmund S. Muskie, then U. S. Senator from Maine, demonstrated this when he spoke to the American Forensic Association in Boston.

"I approach my assignment this morning with many doubts," he said. "In the first place, I am conscious of the professional qualifications of this audience, and question the wisdom of exposing my poor talents to your critical view. In the second place, this is a breakfast meeting—an almost impossible time of day for a man to be on guard effectively; and failure in this respect can be fatal to a politician. And thirdly, there is my subject—the influence which debating has had on my career as a public servant. As long as I am active politically, there is likely to be a sharp division of opinion among my constituents as to whether that influence has been good or bad.

"Facing these doubts, I feel very much like the mosquito who found himself unexpectedly in a nudist colony. I don't know where to begin."

Senator Muskie went on, from there, to make a fine address.

Adlai E. Stevenson played himself down at the beginning of a commencement exercise address at Michigan State University. He said:

"My feeling of inadequacy on these occasions brings to mind Samuel Butler's remark when he was once asked to talk about how to make the most out of life. I think his reply was: 'I don't even know how to make the most out of the next fifteen minutes.' And I feel that way about the next twenty minutes."

The surest way to antagonize an audience is to indicate that you consider yourself to be above them. When you speak, you are in a showcase and every facet of your personality is on display. The slightest hint of braggadocio is fatal. On the other hand, modesty inspires confidence and good will. You can be modest without being apologetic. Your audience will like and respect you for suggesting your limitations as long as you show you are determined to do your best.

The world of American television is a demanding one, and every season top-rated performers fall under the withering fire of competition. One of the survivors who comes back year after year is Ed Sullivan, who is not a television professional, but a newspaper man. He is an amateur in this fiercely competitive field and he survives because he doesn't presume to be anything but an amateur. Some of his mannerisms on camera would have been handicaps for anyone with less natural appeal. He cups his chin in his hand, hunches his shoulders, tugs at his necktie, stumbles over words. But these failings are not fatal for Ed Sullivan. He doesn't resent people for criticizing these faults. At least once a season he hires the services of a talented mimic who caricaturizes him to perfection, exaggerating all his faults. Ed Sullivan laughs as unaffectedly as everyone else when this performer holds the mirror up to nature. He welcomes criticism, and audiences love him for it. Audiences like humility. They resent the show-off, the egotist.

Henry and Dana Lee Thomas, in their book *Living Biographies of Religious Leaders,* said of Confucius:

"He never tried to dazzle people with his exclusive Knowledge. He merely tried to enlighten them with his inclusive sympathy." If we have this inclusive sympathy, we have the key that unlocks the door to the audiences' heart.

> *They may forget what you said, but they will never forget how you made them feel.*
>
> *—Carl W. Buechner*

> *You can make more friends in two months by becoming interested in other people than you can in two years by trying to get other people interested in you.*
>
> *—Dale Carnegie*

PART IV

THE TWO METHODS OF DELIVERING A TALK

Chapter 11

THE SHORT TALK TO GET ACTION

A famous English bishop, during World War I, spoke to the troops at Camp Upton. They were on their way to the trenches; only a very small percentage of them had any adequate idea why they were being sent. I know; I questioned them. Yet the Lord Bishop talked to these men about "International Amity," and "Serbia's Right to a Place in the Sun." Why, half of them did not know whether Serbia was a town or a disease. He might just as well have delivered a learned disquisition on the nebular hypothesis. However, not a single trooper left the hall while he was speaking; military police were stationed at every exit to prevent their escape.

I do not wish to belittle the bishop. He was every inch a scholar, and before a body of churchmen he would probably have been powerful; but he failed with these soldiers, and he failed utterly. Why? He evidently knew neither the precise purpose of his talk nor how to accomplish it.

What do we mean by the purpose of a talk? Just this: every talk, regardless of whether the speaker realizes it or not, has one of four majot goals. What are they?

• • •

1. To persuade or get action.
2. To inform.
3. To impress and convince.
4. To entertain.

Let us illustrate these by a series of concrete examples from Abraham Lincoln's speaking career.

Few people know that Lincoln once invented and patented a device for lifting stranded boats off sand bars and other obstructions. He worked in a mechanic's shop near his law office making a model of his apparatus. When friends came to his office to view the model, he took no end of pains to explain it. The main purpose of those explanations was to inform.

When he delivered his immortal oration at Gettysburg, when he gave his first and second inaugural addresses, when Henry Clay died and Lincoln delivered a eulogy on his life—on all these occasions, Lincoln's main purpose was to impress and convince.

In his talks to juries, he tried to win favorable decisions. In his political talks, he tried to win votes. His purpose, then, was action.

Two years before he was elected president, Lincoln prepared a lecture on inventions. His purpose was to entertain. At least, that should have been his goal; but he was evidently not very successful in attaining it. His career as a popular lecturer was, in fact, a distinct disappointment. In one town, not a person came to hear him.

But he succeeded notably in his other speeches, some of which have become classics of human utterance. Why? Largely because in those instances he knew his goal, and he knew how to achieve it.

Because so many speakers fail to line up their purpose with the purpose of the meeting at which they are speaking, they often flounder and come to grief.

For example: A United States congressman was once hooted and hissed and forced to leave the stage of the old New York Hippodrome, because he had—unconsciously, no doubt, but nevertheless, unwisely—chosen to make an informative talk. The crowd did not want to be instructed. They wanted to be entertained. They listened to him patiently, politely, for ten minutes, a quarter of an hour, hoping the performance would come to a rapid end. But it didn't. He rambled on and on; patience snapped; the audience would not stand for more. Someone began to cheer ironically. Others took it up. In a moment, a thousand people were whistling and shouting. The speaker, obtuse and incapable as he was of sensing the temper of his audience, had the bad taste to continue. That aroused them. A battle was on. Their impatience mounted to ire. They determined to silence him. Louder and louder grew their storm of protest. Finally, the roar of it, the anger of it, drowned his words—he could not have been heard twenty feet away. So he was forced to give up, acknowledge defeat, and retire in humiliation.

Profit by his example. Fit the purpose of your talk to the audience and the occasion. If the congressman had decided in advance whether his goal of informing the audience would fit the goal of the audience in coming to the political rally, he would not have met with disaster. Choose one of the four purposes only after you have analyzed the audience and the occasion which brings them together.

To give you guidance in the important area of speech construction, this entire chapter is devoted to the short talk to get action. The next three chapters will be devoted to the other major speech purposes: to inform, to impress and convince, and to entertain. Each purpose demands a different organizational pattern of treatment, each has its own stumbling blocks that must be hurdled. First, let's get down to the brass tacks of organizing our talks to get the audience to act.

Is there some method of marshaling our material so that we will have the best chance for successful follow-through on what we ask the audience to do? Or is it just a matter of hit-and-miss tactics?

I remember discussing this subject with my associates back in the thirties when my classes were beginning to catch on all over the country. Because of the size of our groups we were using a two-minute limit on the talks given by class members. This limitation did not affect the talk when the purpose of the speaker was merely to entertain or inform. But when we came to the talk to actuate, that was something else. The talk to get action just didn't get off the ground when we used the old system of introduction, body, and conclusion—the organizational pattern followed by speakers since Aristotle. Something new and different was obviously needed to provide us with a sure-fire method of obtaining results in a two-minute talk designed to get action from the listeners.

We held meetings in Chicago, Los Angeles, and New York. We appealed to all our instructors, many of them on the faculties of speech departments in some of our most respected universities. Others were men who held key posts in business administration. Some were from the rapidly expanding field of advertising and promotion. From this amalgam of background and brains, we hoped to get a new approach to speech organization, one that would be streamlined, and one that would reflect our age's need for a psychological as well as a logical method for influencing the listener to act.

We were not disappointed. From those discussions came the Magic Formula of speech construction. We began using it in our classes and we have been using it ever since. What is the Magic Formula? Simply this: Start your talk by giving us the details of your Example, an incident that graphically illustrates the main idea you wish to get across. Second, in specific clearcut terms give your Point, tell exactly what you want your audience to do; and third, give your Reason, that is, highlight the advantage or benefit to be gained by the listener when he does what you ask him to do.

This is a formula highly suited to our swift-paced way of life. Speakers can no longer afford to indulge in long, leisurely introductions. Audiences are composed of busy people who want whatever the speaker has to say in straightforward language. They are accustomed to the digested, boiled-down type of journalism that presents the facts straight from the shoulder. They are exposed to hard-driving Madison Avenue advertising that shoots the message in forceful, clear terms from signboard, television screen, magazine, and newspaper. Every word is measured and nothing is wasted. By using the Magic Formula you can be certain of gaining attention and focusing it upon the main point of your message. It cautions against indulgence in vapid opening remarks, such as: "I didn't have time to prepare this talk very well," or "When your chairman asked me to talk on this subject, I wondered why he selected me." *Audiences are not interested in apologies or excuses, real or simulated.* They want *action.* In the Magic Formula you give them action from the opening word.

The formula is ideal for short talks, because it is based

upon a certain amount of suspense. The listener is caught up in the story you are relating but he is not aware of what the point of your talk is until near the end of the two- or three-minute period. In cases where demands are made upon the audience, this is almost necessary for success. No speaker who wants his audience to dig deep in their pocketbooks for a cause, no matter how worthy, will get very far by starting like this: "Ladies and gentlemen. I'm here to collect five dollars from each of you." There would be a scramble for the exits. But if the speaker describes his visit to the Children's Hospital, where he saw a particularly poignant case of need, a little child who lacked financial help for an operation in a distant hospital, and then asks for contributions, the chances of getting support from his audience would be immeasurably enhanced. It is the story, the *Example,* that prepares the way for the desired action.

Note how the incident-example is used by Leland Stowe to predispose his audience to support the United Nations' Appeal for Children:

I pray that I'll never have to do it again. Can there be anything much worse than to put only a peanut between a child and death? I hope you'll never have to do it, and live with the memory of it afterward. If you had heard their voices and seen their eyes, on that January day in the bomb-scarred workers' district of Athens...Yet all I had left was a half-pound can of peanuts. As I struggled to open it, dozens of ragged kids held me in a vise of frantically clawing bodies. Scores of mothers, with babes in their arms, pushed and fought to get within arm's reach. They held their babies out toward me. Tiny hands of skin and bone stretched convulsively. I tried to make every peanut count.

In their frenzy they nearly swept me off my feet. Nothing but hundreds of hands: begging hands, clutching hands, despairing hands; all of them pitifully little hands. One salted peanut here, and one peanut there. Six peanuts knocked from my fingers, and a savage scramble of emaciated bodies at my feet. Another peanut here, and another peanut there. Hundreds of hands, reaching and pleading; hundreds of eyes with the light of hope flickering out. I stood there helpless, an empty blue can in my hand.... Yes, I hope it will never happen to you.

The Magic Formula can be used also in writing business letters and giving instructions to fellow employees and subordinates. Mothers can use it when motivating their children, and children will find it useful when appealing to their parents for a favor or privilege. You will find it a psychological tool that can be used to get your ideas across to others every day of your life.

Even in advertising, the Magic Formula is used every day. Eveready Batteries recently ran a series of radio and television commercials built upon this Formula. In the Example step, the announcer told of someone's experience of being trapped, for instance, in an overturned car late at night. After giving the graphic details of the accident, he then called upon the victim to finish the story by telling how the beams of the flashlight, powered by Eveready Batteries, brought help in time. Then the announcer went on to the Point and Reason: "Buy Eveready Batteries and you may survive a similar emergency." These stories were all true experiences out of the Eveready Battery Company's files. I don't know how many Eveready Batteries this particular advertising series sold, but I do know that the Magic Formula is an effective method of presenting what you want an audience to do, or to avoid. Let us take up the steps, one at a time.

FIRST

Give Your Example, an Incident from Your Life

This is the part of your talk that will take up the major portion of your time. In it you describe an experience that taught you a lesson. Psychologists say we learn in two ways: one, by the Law of Exercise, in which a series of similar incidents leads to a change of our behavioral patterns; and two, by the Law of Effect, in which a *single* event may be so startling as to cause a change in our conduct. All of us have had this type of unusual experience. We do not have to search long for these incidents because they lie close to the surface of our memories. Our conduct is guided to a latge extent by these experiences. By vividly reconstructing these incidents we can make them the basis of influencing the conduct of others. We can do this because people respond to words in much the same way that they respond to real happenings. In the Example part of your talk, then, you must recreate a segment of your experience in such a way that it tends to have the same effect upon your audience as it originally had upon you. This places upon you the obligation to clarify, intensify, and dramatize your experiences in a way that will make them interesting and compelling to your listeners. Below are a number of suggestions which will help to make the Example step of your action talk clear, intense, and meaningful.

BUILD YOUR EXAMPLE UPON A SINGLE PERSONAL EXPERIENCE

The incident type of example is particularly powerful when it is based upon a single event that had a dramatic impact upon your life. It may not have taken more than a few seconds, but in that short span of time you learned an unforgettable lesson. Not long ago a man in one of our classes told of a terrifying experience when he tried to swim to shore from his overturned boat. I am sure that everyone in his audience made up his mind that, faced with a similar situation, he would follow this speaker's advice and stay with the capsized boat until help came. I remember another example of a speaker's harrowing experience involving a child and an overturned power mower. That incident was so graphically etched in my mind that I will always be on guard when children are hovering near my power mower. Many of our instructors have been so impressed by what they have heard in their classes that they have acted promptly to prevent similar accidents around their homes. One keeps a fire extinguisher handy in his kitchen, for instance, because of a talk he heard which vividly recreated a tragic fire that started from a cooking accident. Another has labeled all bottles containing poison, and has seen to it that they are out of the reach of his children. This action was prompted by a talk detailing the experience of a distraught parent when she discovered her child unconscious in the bathroom with a bottle of poison clutched in her hand.

A single personal experience that taught you a lesson you will never forget is the first requisite of a persuasive action talk. With this kind of incident you can move audiences to act—if it happened to you, your listeners reason, it can happen to them, and they had better take your advice by doing what you ask them to do.

START YOUR TALK WITH A DETAIL OF YOUR EXAMPLE

One of the reasons for starting your talk with the Example step is to catch attention at once. Some speakers fail to get attention with their opening words because all too often these words consist only of repetitious remarks, cliches, or fragmentary apologies that are of no interest to the audience. "Unaccustomed as I am to public speaking," is particularly offensive, but many other commonplace methods of beginning a talk are just as weak in attention-getting value. Going into the details of how you came to choose the subject, revealing to the audience that you are not too well prepared (they will discover that fact soon enough), or announcing the topic or theme of your talk like a preacher giving the text of the sermon are all methods to avoid in the short talk to get action.

Take a tip from top-flight magazine and newspaper writers: begin right in your example and you will capture the attention of your audience immediately.

Here are some opening sentences that drew my attention like a magnet: "In 1942, I found myself on a cot in a hospital"; "Yesterday at breakfast my wife was pouring the coffee and..."; "Last July I was driving at a fast clip down Highway 42..."; "The door of my office opened and Charlie Vann, our foreman, burst in"; "I was fishing in the middle of the lake; I looked up and saw a motor boat speeding toward me."

If you start your talk with phrases that answer one of the questions, Who? When? Where? What? How? or Why?, you will be using one of the oldest communication devices in the world to get attention—the story. "Once upon a time" are the magic words that open the floodgates of a child's imagination. With this same human interest approach you can captivate the minds of your listeners with your first words.

FILL YOUR EXAMPLE WITH RELEVANT DETAIL

Detail, of itself, is not interesting. A room cluttered with furniture and bric-a-brac is not attractive. A picture filled with too many unrelated details does not compel the eyes to linger upon it. In the same way, too many details—unimportant details—make conversation and public speaking a boring test of endurance. The secret is to select only those details that will serve to emphasize the point and reason of the talk. If you want to get across the idea that your listeners should have their cars checked before going on a long trip, then all the details of your Example step should be concerned with what happened to you when you failed to have your car checked before taking a trip. If you tell about how you enjoyed the scenery or where you stayed when you arrived at your destination, you will only succeed in clouding the point and dissipating attention.

But relevant detail, couched in concrete, colorful language, is the best way to recreate the incident as it happened and to picturize it for the audience. To say merely that you once had an accident because of negligence is bald, uninteresting, and hardly likely to move anyone to be more careful behind the wheel of a car. But to paint a word picture of your frightening experience, using the full range of multisensory phraseology, will etch the event upon the consciousness of the listeners. For instance, here is the way one class member developed an Example step that points up vividly the need for great caution on wintry roads:

I was driving north on Highway 41 in Indiana one morning just before Christmas, in 1949. In the car were my wife and two children. For several hours we had been creeping along on a sheet of mirror-like ice; the slightest touch on the steering wheel sent the rear of my Ford into a sickening slide. Few drivers got out of line or attempted to pass, and the hours seemed to creep as slowly as the cars.

Then we came to an open stretch where the ice was melted by the sun and I stepped on the accelerator to make up for lost time. Other cars did the same. Everybody suddenly seemed in a hurry to get to Chicago first. The children began to sing in the back seat as the tension of danger subsided.

The road suddenly went uphill and into a wooded area. As the speeding car reached the top I saw, too late, that the northern slope of the hill, still untouched by the sun's rays, was like a smooth river of ice. I had a fleeting glance of two wildly careening cars in front of us and then we went into a skid. Over the shoulder we went, hopelessly out of control, and landed in a snowbank, still upright; but the car that had been following us went into a skid, too, and crashed into the side of our car, smashing in the doors and showering us with glass.

The abundance of detail in this example made it easy for the audience to project themselves into the picture. After all, your purpose is to make your audience see what you saw, hear what you heard, feel what you felt. The only way you can possibly achieve this effect is to use an abundance of concrete details. As was pointed out in Chapter Four, the task of preparation of a talk is a task of reconstructing the answers to the questions Who? When? Where? How? and Why? You must stimulate the visual imagination of your listeners by painting word pictures.

RELIVE YOUR EXPERIENCE AS YOU RELATE IT

In addition to using picturesque details, the speaker should relive the experience he is describing. Here is where speaking approaches its sister field of acting. All great speakers have a sense of the dramatic, but this is not a rare quality, to be found only in the eloquent. Most children have a plentiful supply of it. Many persons of our acquaintance are gifted with a sense of timing, facial expression, mimicry, or pantomime that is a part, at least, of this priceless ability to dramatize. Most of us have some skill along these lines, and with a little effort and practice we can develop more of it.

The more action and excitement you can put into the retelling of your incident, the more it will make an impression on your listeners. No matter how rich in detail a talk may be, it will lack punch if the speaker does not give it with all the fervor of re-creation. Are you describing a fire?

Give us the feeling of excitement that ran through the crowd as the firemen battled the blaze. Are you telling us about an argument with your neighbor? Relive it; dramatize it. Are you relating your final struggles in the water as panic swept over you? Make your audience feel the desperation of those awful moments in your life. For one of the purposes of the example is to make your talk memorable. Your listener will remember your talk and what you want them to do only if the example sticks in their minds. We recall George Washington's honesty because of the cherry tree incident popularized in the Weem's biography. The New Testament is a rich storehouse of principles of ethical conduct reinforced by examples full of human interest—for instance, the story of the Good Samaritan.

In addition to making your talk more easily remembered, the incident-example makes your talk more interesting, more convincing, and easier to understand. Your experience of what life has taught you is freshly perceived by the audience: they are in a sense, predetermined to respond to what you want them to do. This brings us right to the doorstep of the second phase of the Magic Formula.

SECOND

State Your Point, What You Want the Audience to Do

The Example step of your talk to get action has consumed more than three-quarters of your time. Assume you are talking for two minutes. You have about twenty seconds in which to hammer home the desired action you wish the audience to take and the benefit they can expect as a result of doing what you ask. The need for detail is over. The time for forthright, direct assertion has come. It is the reverse of the newspaper technique. Instead of giving the headline first, you give the news story and then you headline it with your Point or appeal for action. This step is governed by three rules:

MAKE THE POINT BRIEF AND SPECIFIC

Be precise in telling the audience exactly what you want them to do. People will do only what they clearly understand. It is essential to ask yourself just exactly what it is you want the audience to do now that they have been disposed to action by your example. It is a good idea to write the point out as you would a telegram, trying to reduce the number of words and to make your language as clear and explicit as possible. Don't say: "Help the patients in our local orphanage." That's too general. Say instead: "Sign up tonight to meet next Sunday to take twenty-five children on a picnic." It is important to ask for an overt action, one that can be seen, rather than mental actions, which are too vague. For instance, "Think of your grandparents now and then," is too general to be acted upon. Say instead: "Make a point of visiting your grandparents this weekend." A statement such as, "Be patriotic," should be converted into "Cast your vote next Tuesday."

MAKE THE POINT EASY FOR LISTENERS TO DO

No matter what the issue is, controversial or otherwise, it is the speaker's responsibility to word his point, the request for action, in such a way that it will be easy for his listeners to understand and to do. One of the best ways to do this is to be specific. If you want your listeners to improve their ability to remember names, don't say: "Start now to improve your memory of names." That is so general it is difficult to do. Say instead; "Repeat the name of the next stranger you meet five times within five minutes after you meet him."

Speakers who give detailed action points are more apt to be successful in motivating their audiences than those who rest upon generalities. To say: "Sign the get well card in the back of the room" is far better than to urge your listeners to send a card or write a letter to a hospitalized fellow class member.

The question whether to state the point negatively or positively should be answered by looking at it from the listeners' point of view. Not all negatively phrased points are ineffective. When they epitomize an avoidance attitude they are probably more convincing to listeners than a positively stated appeal. Don't be a bulb-snatcher was an avoidance phrase employed with great effect some years ago in an advertising campaign designed to sell electric light bulbs.

STATE THE POINT WITH FORCE AND CONVICTION

The Point is the entire theme of your talk. You should give it, therefore, with forcefulness and conviction. As a headline stands out in block letters, your request for action should be emphasized by vocal animation and directness. You are about to make your last impression on the audience. Make it in such a way that the audience feels the sincerity of your appeal for action. There should be no uncertainty or diffidence about the way you ask for the order. This persuasiveness of manner should carry over to your last words, in which you give the third step of the Magic Formula.

THIRD

Give the Reason or Benefit the Audience May Expect

Here again, brevity and economy are necessary. In the reason step you hold out the incentive or reward the listeners may expect if they do what you have asked in the Point.

BE SURE THE REASON IS RELEVANT TO THE EXAMPLE

Much has been written about motivation in public speaking. It is a vast subject and a useful one for anyone engaged in persuading others to act. In the short talk to get action, on which we are centering our attention in this chapter, all you can hope to do is highlight the benefit in a sentence or two and then sit down. It is most important, however, that you focus upon the benefit that was brought out in the Example step. If you tell of your experience in saving money by buying a used car, and urge your listeners to buy a secondhand car, you must emphasize in your reason that they, too, may enjoy the economical advantages of buying secondhand. You should not deviate from the example by giving as your reason the fact that some used cars have better styling than the latest models.

BE SURE TO STRESS ONE REASON—AND ONE ONLY

Most salesmen can give a half-dozen reasons why you should buy their product, and it is quite possible that you can give several reasons to back up your Point and all of them may be relevant to the Example you used. But again it is best to choose one outstanding reason or benefit and rest your case on it Your final words to the audience should be as clear-cut as the message on an advertisement in a national magazine. If you study these ads upon which so much talent has been expended, you will develop skill in handling the point and reason of your talk. No ad attempts to sell more than one product or one idea at a time. Very few ads in the big circulation magazines use more than one reason why you should buy. The same company may change its motivational appeal from one medium to another, from television to newspapers, for instance, but rarely will the same company make different appeals in one ad, whether vocal or visual.

If you study the ads you see in magazines and newspapers and on television and analyze their content you will be amazed at how often the Magic Formula is used to persuade people to buy. You will become aware of the ribbon of relevancy which binds the whole ad or commercial together into a unified package.

There are other ways of building up an example, for instance, by using exhibits, giving a demonstration, quoting authorities, making comparisons, and citing statistics. These will be explained more at length in Chapter Thirteen, where the longer talk to persuade will be discussed. In this chapter, the formula has been restricted to the personal incident type of example because, in the short talk to get action, it is by far the easiest and most interesting, dramatic, and persuasive method a speaker can use.

No one ever complains about a speech being too short!

—Ira Hayes

Your purpose is to make your audience see what you saw, hear what you heard, feel what you felt. Relevant detail, couched in concrete, colourful language, is the best way to recreate the incident as it happened and to picture it for the audience.

—Dale Carnegie

Chapter 12

THE TALK TO INFORM

Probably you often have heard speakers like one who once made a United States Senate investigating committee squirm with annoyance. He was a high-ranking government official, but he did not know any better than to talk on and on, vaguely, without ever making his meaning clear. He was pointless and obscure, and the committee's confusion mounted by the moment. Finally one of its members, Samuel James Ervin, Jr., speaking as the senior Senator from North Carolina, got a chance to say a few words—and they were telling ones.

He said the official reminded him of a husband he knew back home. The husband notified his lawyer he wanted to divorce his wife, although he conceded she was beautiful, a fine cook, and a model mother.

"They why do you want to divorce her?" his lawyer asked. "Because she talks all the time," the husband replied. "What does she talk about?"

"That's the trouble," the husband answered, "she never says!"

This is the trouble, too, with many speakers, both women and men. Their hearers don't know what such speakers are talking about. They never say. They never make their meaning clear.

In Chapter Seven, you received a formula for making short talks to get action from your listeners. Now, I am going to give you methods to help make your meaning clear when you set out to inform, and not motivate, your listeners.

We make informative talks many times every day: giving directions or instructions, making explanations and reports. Of all the types of talks given every week to audiences everywhere, the talk to inform is second only to the talk to persuade or get action. The ability to speak clearly precedes the ability to move others to action. Owen D. Young, one of. America's top industrialists, emphasizes the need for clear expression in today's world:

As one enlarges his ability to get others to understand him, he opens up to that extent his opportunity for usefulness. Certainly in our society, where it is necessary for men even in the simplest matters to co-operate with each other, it is necessary for them first of all to understand each other. Language is the principal conveyor of understanding, and so we must learn to use it, not crudely but discriminatingly.

In this chapter are some suggestions to help you see language so clearly and discriminately that your audience will have no difficulty understanding you. "Everything that can be thought at all," said Ludwig Wittgenstein, "can be thought clearly. Everything that can be said, can be said clearly."

FIRST

Restrict Your Subject to Fit the Time at Your Disposal

In one of his talks to teachers, Professor William James

pauses to remark that one can make only one point in a lecture, and the lecture he referred to lasted an hour. Yet I recently heard a speaker, who was limited by a stop watch to three minutes, begin by saying that he wanted to call our attention to eleven points. Sixteen and a half seconds to each phase of his subject! Seems incredible, doesn't it, that an intelligent man should attempt anything so manifestly absurd? True, this is an extreme case but the tendency to err in that fashion, if not to that degree, handicaps almost every novice. He is like a Cook's guide who shows Paris to the tourist in one day. It can be done, just as one can walk through the American Museum of Natural History in thirty minutes. But neither clearness nor enjoyment results. Many a talk fails to be clear because the speaker seems intent upon establishing a world's record for ground covered in the allotted time. He leaps from one point to another with the swiftness and agility of a mountain goat

If, for example, yon are to speak on Labor Unions, do not attempt to tell us in three or six minutes why they came into existence, the methods they employ, the good they have accomplished, the evil they have wrought, and how to solve industrial disputes. No, no; if you strive to do that, no one will have a very clear conception of what you have said. It will be all confused, a blur, too sketchy, too much of a mere outline.

Wouldn't it be the part of wisdom to take one phase, and one phase only, of labor unions, and cover that adequately and illustrate it? It would. That kind of talk leaves a single impression. It is lucid, easy to listen to, easy to remember.

When I went to call one morning on a company president whom I know, I found a strange name on his door. The personnel director, an old friend of mine, told me why.

"His name caught up with him," my friend said.

"His name?" I repeated. "He was one of the Joneses who

control the company, wasn't he?"

"I mean his nickname," my friend said. "It was `Where-Is-He-Now?' Everyone called him 'Where-Is He-Now' Jones. He didn't last long. The family put a cousin in his place. He never took the pains to know what this business is all about. He'd put in a good long day, all right, but doing what? Popping in here, popping in there, all over the place, all the time. Just sort of covering ground. He thought it was more important for him to see that a shipping clerk turned out an electric light or that a stenographer picked up a paper clip than it was for him to study a big sales campaign. He wasn't in his office much. That's why we called him 'Where-Is-He-Now.' "

"Where-Is-He-Now" Jones reminds me of many speakers who could do much better than they do. They don't do better because they won't discipline themselves. They are the ones who, like Mr. Jones, try to cover too much ground. Haven't you heard them? And in the midst of a talk, haven't you wondered, "Where is he now?"

Even some experienced speakers are guilty of this fault. Perhaps the fact that they are capable in many other ways blinds them to the danger in dispersed effort. You need not be like them. Hold fast to your main theme. If you are to make yourself clear, your hearers must always be able to say, "I understand him. I know where he is now!"

SECOND

Arrange Your Ideas in Sequence

Almost all subjects can be developed by using a logical sequence based on time, space, or special topics. In the time sequence, for instance, you might consider your subject under the three categories of past, present, and future, or you might begin at a certain date and move backward or forward from that date. All process talks, for example, should begin at the raw-material stage and move through the various manufacturing steps that produce the finished product. How much detail you bring in will, of course, be governed by the time you have.

In the space sequence, you arrange your ideas according to some central point and go outward from there or you cover the material directionally, north, south, east, and west. If you were to describe the city of Washington, D. C., you might take your listeners to the top of the capitol building and indicate the points of interest in each direction. If you are describing a jet engine or an automobile, for example, you might best discuss it by breaking it down into its component parts.

Some subjects have a built-in sequence. If you set out to explain the structure of the United States Government, you will do well to follow this inherent organizational pattern and discuss it according to the legislative, executive, and judicial branches.

THIRD

Enumerate Your Points as You Make Them

One of the simplest ways to keep a talk shipshape in the minds of your listeners is to mention plainly as you go along that you are taking up first one point and then another.

"My first point is this... " You can be as blunt as that. When you've discussed the point, you can say frankly that you are going to the second one. You can keep on that way to the end.

Dr. Ralph J. Bunche, when assistant secretary-general of the United Nations, began an important talk sponsored by the City Club of Rochester, New York, in this straightforward manner:

"I have chosen to speak tonight on the topic 'The

Challenge of Human Relations,' for two reasons," he said. He went on at once to add, "In the first place...." He continued soon, "In the second place...." Throughout the talk, he was careful to make clear to his audience that he was leading it, point by point, to his conclusion:

"We must never lose faith in man's potential power for good."

The same method was given an effective twist when the economist, Paul H. Douglas, spoke to a congressional joint committee struggling with means to stimulate business when it once was lagging in this country. He spoke both as a tax expert and as Senator from Illinois.

"My theme," he began, "is this: The quickest and most effective way to act is by means of a tax cut for lower and middle income groups–that is, those groups which tend to spend almost all their income."

"Specifically...," he went on.

"Further...," he continued.

"In addition...," he continued.

"There are three principal reasons: First...Second... Third...

"In summation, what we need is an immediate tax cut for low and middle income groups in order to increase demand and purchasing power."

FOURTH

Compare the Strange with the Familiar

Sometimes you will find yourself floundering in a vain attempt to explain your meaning. It's something quite clear to you but requiring involved explanation if your hearers are to be clear about it too. What to do? Compare it with something your hearers do understand; say one thing is like the other, the strange like the familiar.

Suppose you are discussing one of chemistry's contributions to industry—a catalyst. It is a substance that causes changes to occur in other substances without changing itself. That's fairly simple. But isn't this better? It is like a little boy in a schoolyard, tripping, punching, upsetting, poking all the other children there, and never being touched by a blow from anyone else.

Some missionaries once had to face this problem of putting strange statements into familiar terms when they translated the Bible into the dialect of a tribe living in equatorial Africa. Should they translate literally? They realized that if they did, the words at times would be meaningless to the natives.

They came, for example, to the lines: "Though your sins be as scarlet, they shall be white as snow." Should they translate this literally? The natives didn't know snow from jungle moss. But they had often climbed coconut trees and had shaken down nuts for lunch. The missionaries likened the unknown to the known. They changed the lines to read:

"Though your sins be as scarlet, they shall be white as the meat of a coconut."

Under the circumstances, it would be hard to improve on that, wouldn't it?

TURN A FACT INTO A PICTURE

How far away is the moon? The sun? The nearest other star? Scientists are apt to answer space-travel questions with a lot of mathematics. But science lecturers and writers know this is no way to make a fact clear to an average audience. They turn the figures into pictures.

The famous scientist Sir James Jeans was particularly

interested in mankind's yearnings to explore the universe. As a scientific expert, he knew the mathematics involved, and he also knew that he would be most effective in writing or speaking if he dropped in a figure only here and there.

Our sun (a star) and the planets around us are so near that we do not realize how far away other objects whirling in space are, he pointed out in his book, *The Universe Around Us*. "Even the nearest star (Proxima Centauri) is 25,000,000,000,000 miles away," he said. Then, to make this figure more vivid, he explained that if one were to take off from the earth at the speed of light-186,000 miles a second—it would take him four and a quarter years to reach Proxima Centauri.

In this way, he made the vast distances in space seem more real than did another speaker whom I once heard describe such a simple thing as distances in Alaska. He said Alaska's area was 590,804 square miles, and dropped the attempt to show its size right there.

Does this give you any kind of picture of the size of the 49th State? It didn't give me one. To visualize its bigness, I had to wait until I learned from another source that its area more than equals the combined areas of Vermont, New Hampshire, Maine, Massachusetts, Rhode Island, Connecticut, New York, New Jersey, Pennsylvania, Delaware, Maryland, West Virginia, North Carolina, South Carolina, Georgia, Florida, Tennessee, and Mississippi. Now the 590,804 square miles take on a new meaning, don't they? You realize that in Alaska there's plenty of room to move around.

Some years ago a member of one of our classes described the fearful toll of fatal accidents on our highways by this appalling picture: "You are driving across the country from New York to Los Angeles. Instead of highway markers, imagine coffins standing upright in the earth, each containing a victim of last year's slaughter on the roads. As you speed along your car passes one of these gruesome markers every five seconds, for they are spaced twelve to a mile from one end of the country to the other!"

I never take a ride in a car very far before that picture comes back to me with startling realism.

Why is that so? Because ear impressions are hard to retain. They roll away like sleet striking the smooth bark of a beech tree. But eye impressions? I saw, a few years ago, a cannon ball imbedded in an old house standing on the banks of the Danube—a cannon ball that Napoleon's artillery had fired at the battle of Ulm. Visual impressions are like that cannon ball; they come with a terrific impact. They imbed themselves. They stick. They tend to drive out all opposing suggestions as Bonaparte drove away the Austrians.

AVOID TECHNICAL TERMS

If you belong to a profession the work of which is technical—if you are a lawyer, a physician, an engineer, or are in a highly specialized line of business— be doubly careful, when you talk to outsiders, to express yourself in plain terms and to give necessary details.

Be doubly careful, for, as a part of my professional duties, I have listened to hundreds of speeches that failed right at this point, and failed woefully. The speakers appeared totally unconscious of the general public's widespread and profound ignorance regarding their particular specialties. So what happened? They rambled on and on, uttering thoughts, using phrases that fitted into their experience and were instantly and continuously meaningful to them; but to the uninitiated, they were about as clear as the Missouri River after the June rains have fallen on the newly plowed cornfields of Iowa and Kansas.

What should such a speaker do? He ought to read and

heed the following advice from the facile pen of former Senator Beveridge of Indiana:

It is a good practice to pick out the least intelligent-looking person in the audience and strive to make that person interested in your argument. This can be done only by lucid statements of fact and clear reasoning. An even better method is to center your talk on some small boy or girl present with parents.

Say to yourself—say out loud to your audience, if you like—that you will try to be so plain that the child will understand and remember your explanation of the question discussed, and after the meeting be able to tell what you have said.

A physician in one of our classes remarked in a talk that "diaphragmatic breathing is a distinct aid to the peristaltic action of the intestines and a boon to health." He was about to dismiss that phase of his talk with that one sentence and to rush on to something else. The instructor stopped him, and asked for a show of hands of those who had a clear conception of how diaphragmatic breathing differs from other kinds of breathing, why it is especially beneficial to physical well-being, and what peristaltic action is. The result of the vote surprised the doctor; so he went back, explained, enlarged in this fashion:

The diaphragm is a thin muscle forming the floor of the chest at the base of the lungs and the roof of the abdominal cavity. When inactive and during chest breathing, it is arched like an inverted washbowl.

In abdominal breathing every breath forces this muscular arch down until it becomes nearly flat and you can feel your stomach muscles pressing against your belt. This downward pressure of the diaphragm massages and stimulates the organs of the upper part of the abdominal cavity—the stomach, the liver, the pancreas, the spleen, the solar plexus.

When you breathe out again, your stomach and your intestines will be forced up against the diaphragm and will be given another massage. This massaging helps the process of elimination.

A vast amount of ill health originates in the intestines. Most indigestion, constipation, and autointoxication would disappear if our stomachs and intestines were properly exercised through deep diaphragmatic breathing.

It is always best to go from the simple to the complex in giving explanations of any kind. For example, suppose you were trying to explain to a group of housewives why refrigerators must be defrosted. This would be the wrong way to go about it:

The principle of refrigeration is based on the fact that the evaporator pulls heat from the inner portion of the refrigerator. As the heat is pulled out, the accompanying humidity clings to the evaporator, piling up into a thickness which insulates the evaporator and necessitates more frequent turning on of the motor to compensate for the thickening frost.

Notice how much easier it is to understand if the speaker starts with what the housewives are familiar with:

You know where you freeze meat in your refrigerator. Well, you know, too, how the frost gathers on that freezer. Every day the frost gets thicker and thicker until the freezer must be defrosted to keep the refrigerator in good working order. You see, frost around the freezer is really like a blanket covering you in bed or like rock wool between the walls insulating your house. Now the thicker the frost gets, the harder it is for the freezer to pull the warm air out of the rest of the refrigerator and keep the refrigerator cold. The refrigerator motor then must work more often and longer to keep the box cold. But with an automatic defroster on your refrigerator, the frost never gets a chance to build up thickly. Consequently, the motor works less often and for shorter periods.

Aristotle gave some good advice on the subject: "Think as wise men do, but speak as the common people do." If you must use a technical term, don't use it until you have explained it so everybody in the audience knows what it means. This is especially true of your keystone words, the ones you use over and over.

I once heard a stockbroker speak to a group of women who wanted to learn fundamentals of banking and investment. He used simple language and he put them at ease in a conversational way. He made everything clear except his foundation words, which were strange to them. He spoke of the "clearing house," "puts and calls," "refunding mortgages," and "short sales and long sales." What could have been a fascinating discussion became a puzzle because he did not realize his hearers were unfamiliar with the words that were part and parcel of his trade.

There is no reason to avoid a keystone word which you know will not be understood. Just explain it as soon as you use it. Never fail to do this; the dictionary is all yours.

Do you want to say something about singing commercials? Or about impulse buying? About liberal arts courses, or cost accounting? About government subsidies, or automobiles that pass on the wrong side? Would you like to advocate a permissive attitude toward children, or the LIFO system of valuing inventories? Merely make sure that your hearers accept your keystone words in these specialized fields in the same sense in which you accept them.

FIFTH

Use Visual Aids

The nerves that lead from the eye to the brain are many times larger than those leading from the ear; and science tells us that we give twenty-five times as much attention to eye suggestions as we do to ear suggestions.

"One seeing," says an old Japanese proverb, "is better than a hundred times telling about."

So, if you wish to be clear, picture your points, visualize your ideas. That was the plan of John H. Patterson, founder of the National Cash Register Company. He wrote an article for *System Magazine,* outlining the methods he used in speaking to his workmen and his sales forces:

> I hold that one cannot rely on speech alone to make himself understood or to gain and hold attention. A dramatic supplement is needed. It is better to supplement whenever possible with pictures which show the right and the wrong way: diagrams are more convincing than mere words, and pictures are more convincing than diagrams. The ideal presentation of a subject is one in which every subdivision is pictured and in which the words are used only to connect them. I early found that in dealing with men, a picture was worth more than anything I could say.

If you use a chart or diagram, be sure it is large enough to see, and don't overdo a good thing. A long succession of charts is usually boring. If you make the diagram as you go along, be careful to sketch roughly and swiftly on the blackboard or flip chart. Listeners are not interested in great art work. Use abbreviations; write largely and legibly; keep talking as you draw or write; and keep turning back to your audience.

When you use exhibits, follow these suggestions and you will be assured of the rapt attention of your audience.

Keep the exhibit out of sight until you are ready to use it.

Use exhibits large enough to be seen from the very last row. Certainly your audience can't learn from any exhibit unless they see it.

Never pass an exhibit around among your listeners while you are speaking. Why invite competition?

When you show an exhibit, hold it up where your listeners can see it.

Remember, one exhibit that moves is worth ten that don't. Demonstrate if practicable.

Don't stare at the exhibit as you talk—you are trying to communicate with the audience, not with the exhibit.

When you have finished with the exhibit, get it out of sight if practicable.

If the exhibit you are going to use lends itself to "mystery treatment," have it placed on a table which will be at your side as you speak. Have it covered. As you talk, make references to it that will arouse curiosity—but don't tell what it is. Then, when you are ready to unveil it, you have aroused curiosity, suspense, and real interest.

Visual materials are becoming more and more prominent as devices to promote clarity. There is no better way to insure that your audience will understand what you have to say than to go before them prepared to show as well as to tell them what you have in mind.

Two American presidents, both masters of the spoken word, have indicated that the ability to be clear is the result of training and discipline. As Lincoln said, we must have a passion for clarity. He told Dr. Gulliver, the President of Knox College, how he developed this "passion" in early life:

Among my earliest recollections I remember how, when a mere child, I used to get irritated when anybody talked to me in a way I could not understand. I don't think I ever got angry at anything else in my life. But that always disturbed my temper, and has ever since. I can remember going to my little bedroom, after hearing the neighbors talk of an evening with my father, and spending no small part of the night walking up and down and trying to make out the exact meaning of some of their, to me, dark sayings. I could not sleep, though I often tried to, when I got on such a hunt after an idea, until I had repeated it over and over, until I had put it in language plain enough as I thought for any boy I knew to comprehend. This was a kind of passion with me, and it has since stuck by me.

The other distinguished president, Woodrow Wilson, wrote some words of advice that strike the right note to end this chapter on making your meaning clear:

My father was a man of great intellectual energy. My best training came from him. He was intolerant of vagueness, and from the time I began to write until his death in 1903, when he was eighty-one years old, I carried everything I wrote to him. He would make me read it aloud, which was always painful to me. Every now and then, he would stop me. "What do you mean by that?" I would tell him, and, of course, in doing so would express myself more simply than I had on paper. "Why didn't you say so?" he would go on. "Don't shoot at your meaning with birdshot and hit the whole countryside; shoot with a rifle at the thing you have to say."

He who wants to persuade should put his trust not in the right argument, but in the right word. The power of sound has always been greater than the power of sense.

—Joseph Conrad

Applause is a receipt, not a bill.

—Dale Carnegie

Chapter 13

THE TALK TO CONVINCE

There was once a small group of men and women who found themselves in the path of a hurricane. Not a real hurricane, but the next thing to it. In short, a hurricane of a man named Maurice Goldblatt. Here is how one of that group described it:

We were sitting around a luncheon table in Chicago. We knew this man was reputed to be a powerful speaker. We watched him intently as he stood up to speak.

He began quietly—a spruce, pleasant man of middle age—thanking us for inviting him. He wanted to talk about something serious, he said, and he hoped we would forgive him if he disturbed us.

Then, like a whirlwind, he struck. He leaned forward and his eyes transfixed us. He didn't raise his voice, but it seemed to me that it crashed like a gong.

"Look around you," he said. "Look at one another. Do you know how many of you sitting now in this room are going to die of cancer? One in four of all of you who are over forty-five. One in four!"

He paused, and his face lightened. “That’s a plain, harsh fact, but it needn’t be for long,” he said. “Something can be done about it. This something is progress in the treatment of cancer and in the search for its cause.”

He looked at us gravely, his gaze moving around the table. “Do you want to help toward this progress?” he asked.

Could there have been an answer except “Yes!” in the minds of any of us then? “Yes!” I thought, and I found later that so did the others.

In less than a minute, Maurice Goldblatt had won us. He had drawn us personally into his subject. He had us on his side, in the campaign he was waging for a humanitarian cause.

Getting a favorable reaction is every speaker’s objective any time, anywhere. As it happened, Mr. Goldblatt had a dramatically good reason for wanting to get one from us. He and his brother, Nathan, starting with little more than nothing, had built up a department store chain doing a business of more than $100,000,000 a year. Fabulous success had come to them after long, hard years, and then Nathan, ill only a short time, had died of cancer. After that, Maurice Goldblatt saw to it that the Goldblatt Foundation gave the first million dollars to the University of Chicago’s cancer research program, and he gave his own time—retiring from business—to the work of interesting the public in the fight against cancer.

These facts, together with Maurice Goldblatt’s personality, won us. Sincerity, earnestness, enthusiasm—a blazing determination to give himself to us for a few minutes, just as he was giving himself year in and out to a great cause—all of these factors swept us up into a feeling of agreement with the speaker, a friendliness for him, a willingness to be interested and moved.

FIRST

Win Confidence by Deserving It

Quintilian described the orator as "a good man skilled in speaking." He was talking about sincerity and character. Nothing said in this book, nor anything which will be said, can take the place of this essential attribute of speaking effectiveness. Pierpont Morgan said that character was the best way to obtain credit; it is also the best way to win the confidence of the audience.

"The sincerity with which a man speaks," said Alexander Woolcott, "imparts to his voice a color of truth no perjurer can feign."

Especially when the purpose of our talk is to convince, it is necessary to set forth our own ideas with the inner glow that comes from sincere conviction. We must first be convinced before we attempt to convince others.

SECOND

Get a Yes-Response

Walter Dill Scott, former president of Northwestern University, said that "every idea, concept, or conclusion which enters the mind is held as true unless hindered by some contradictory idea." That boils down to keeping the audience yes-minded. My good friend Professor Harry Overstreet brilliantly examined the psychological background of this concept in a lecture at the New School for Social Research in New York City:

The skillful speaker gets at the outset a number of yes-responses. He has thereby set the psychological processes of his listeners moving in the affirmative direction. It is like the movement of a billiard ball. Propel it in one direction, and it takes some force to deflect it, far more force to send it back in the opposite direction.

The psychological patterns here are quite clear.

When a person says "No" and really means it, he is doing far more than saying a word of two letters. His entire organism—glandular, nervous, muscular—gathers itself together into a condition of rejection. There is, usually in minute but sometimes in observable degree, a physical withdrawal, or readiness for withdrawal. The whole neuromuscular system, in short, sets itself on guard against acceptance. Where, on the contrary, a person says "Yes," none of the withdrawing activities takes place. The organism is in a forward-moving, accepting, open attitude. Hence the more "Yesses" we can, at the very outset, induce, the more likely we are to succeed in capturing the attention for our ultimate proposal.

It is a very simple technique—this yes-response. And yet how much neglected! It often seems as if people get a sense of their own importance by antagonizing at the outset. The radical comes into a conference with his conservative brethren; and immediately he must make them furious! What, as a matter of fact, is the good of it? If he simply does it in order to get some pleasure out of it for himself, he may be pardoned. But if he expects to achieve something, he is only psychologically stupid.

Get a student to say "No" at the beginning, or a customer, child, husband, or wife, and it takes the wisdom and patience of angels to transform that bristling negative into an affirmative.

How is one going to get these desirable "yes-responses" at the very outset? Fairly simple. "My way of opening and winning an argument," confided Lincoln, "is to first find a common ground of agreement." Lincoln found it even when he was discussing the highly inflammable subject of slavery. "For the first half hour," declared *The Mirror,* a neutral paper reporting one of his talks, "his opponents would agree with every word he uttered. From that point he began to lead them off, little by little, until it seemed as if he had got them all into his fold."

Is it not evident that the speaker who argues with his audience is merely arousing their stubbornness, putting them on the defensive, making it well-nigh impossible for them to change their minds? Is it wise to start by saying, "I am going to prove so and so"? Aren't your hearers liable to accept that as a challenge and remark silently, "Let's see you do it"?

Is it not much more advantageous to begin by stressing something that you and all of your hearers believe, and then to raise some pertinent question that everyone would like to have answered? Then take your audience with you in an earnest search for the answer. While on that search, present the facts as you see them so clearly that they will be led to accept your conclusions as their own. They will have much more faith in some truth that they have discovered for themselves. "The best argument is that which seems merely an explanation."

In every controversy, no matter how wide and bitter the differences, there is always some common ground of agreement on which a speaker can invite everyone to meet. To illustrate: On February 3, 1960, the prime minister of Great Britain, Harold Macmillan, addressed both houses of the Parliament of the Union of South Africa. He had to present the United Kingdom's nonracial viewpoint before the legislature body at a time when apartheid was the prevailing policy Did he begin his talk with this essential difference in outlook? No. He began by stressing the great economic progress made by South Africa, the significant contributions made by South Africa to the world. Then, with skill and tact he brought up the questions of differing viewpoints. Even here, he indicated that he was well aware that these differences were based on sincere conviction. His whole talk was a masterly statement reminding one of Lincoln's gentle but firm utterances in the years before Fort Sumter. "As a fellow member of the Commonwealth," said the Prime Minister, "it is our earnest desire to give South Africa our support and encouragement, but I hope you won't mind my saying frankly that there are some aspects of your policies which make it impossible for us to do this without being false to our deep convictions about the political destinies of free men to which in our own territories we are trying to give effect. I think we ought as friends to face together, without seeking to apportion credit or blame, the fact that in the world of today this difference of outlook lies between us."

No matter how determined one was to differ with a speaker, a statement like that would tend to convince you of the speaker's fair-mindedness.

What would have been the result had Prime Minister Macmillan set out immediately to emphasize the difference in policy rather than the common ground of agreement? Professor James Harvey Robinson's enlightening book, *The Mind in the Making,* gives the psychological answer to that question:

We sometimes find ourselves changing our minds without any resistance or heavy emotion, but if we are told we are wrong we resent the imputation and harden our hearts. We are incredibly heedless in the formation of our beliefs, but find ourselves filled with an illicit passion for them when anyone proposes to rob us of their companionship. It is obviously not the ideas themselves that are dear to us, but our self-esteem which is threatened... The little word *my* is the most important one in human affairs, and properly to reckon with it is the beginning of wisdom. It has the same force whether it is *my* dinner, *my* dog, and my house, or my faith, *my* country and my God. We not only resent the imputation that our watch is wrong, or our car shabby, but that our conception of the canals of Mars, of the pronunciation of "Epictetus," of the medicinal value of salicine, or of the date of Sargon I, are subject to revision... We like to continue to believe what we have been accustomed to accept as true, and the resentment aroused when doubt is cast upon any of our assumptions leads us to seek every manner of excuse for clinging to it. The result is that most of our so-called reasoning consists in finding arguments for going on believing as we already do.

THIRD

Speak with Contagious Enthusiasm

Contradicting ideas are much less likely to arise in the listener's mind when the speaker presents his ideas with feeling and contagious enthusiasm. I say "contagious," for enthusiasm is just that. It thrusts aside all negative and opposing ideas. When your aim is to convince, remember it is more productive to stir emotions than to arouse thoughts. Feelings are more powerful than cold ideas. To arouse feelings one must be intensely in earnest. Regardless of the petty phrases a man may concoct, regardless of the illustrations he may assemble, regardless of the harmony of his voice and the grace of his gestures, if he does not speak sincerely, these are hollow and glittering trappings. If you would impress an audience, be impressed yourself. Your spirit, shining through your eyes, radiating through your voice, and proclaiming itself through your manner, will communicate itself to your audience.

Every time you speak, and especially when your avowed purpose is to convince, what you do determines the attitude of your listeners. If you are lukewarm, so will they be; if you are flippant and antagonistic, so will they be. "When the congregation falls asleep," wrote Henry Ward Beecher, "there is only one thing to do; provide the usher with a sharp stick and have him prod the preacher."

I was once one of three judges called on to award the Curtis medal at Columbia University. There were half a dozen undergraduates, all of them elaborately trained, all of them eager to acquit themselves well. But—with only a single exception—what they were striving for was to win the medal. They had little or no desire to convince.

They had chosen their topics because these topics permitted oratorical development. They had no deep personal interest in the arguments they were making. And their successive talks were merely exercises in the art of delivery.

The exception was a. Zulu Prince. He had selected as his theme "The Contribution of Africa to Modern Civilization." He put intense feeling into every word he uttered. His talk was no mere exercise; it was a living thing, born of conviction and enthusiasm. He spoke as the representative of his people, of his continent; with wisdom, high character, and good will, he brought us a message of his people's hopes and a plea for our understanding.

We gave him the medal although he was possibly no more accomplished in addressing a large group than two or three of his competitors. What we judges recognized was that his talk had the true fire of sincerity; it was ablaze with truth. Beside it, the other talks were only flickering gas-logs.

The Prince had learned in his own way in a distant land that you can't project your personality in a talk to others by using reason alone: you have to reveal to them how deeply you yourself believe in what you say.

FOURTH

Show Respect and Affection for Your Audience

"The human personality demands love and it also demands respect," Dr. Norman Vincent Peale said as a prelude to speaking of a professional comedian. "Every human being has an inner sense of worth, of importance, of dignity. Wound that and you have lost that person forever. So when you love and respect a person you build him up and, accordingly, he loves and esteems you.

"At one time I was on a program with an entertainer. I did not know the man well, but since that meeting I read that he was having difficulty, and I think I know why.

"I had been sitting beside him quietly for I was about to speak. 'You aren't nervous, are you?' he asked

" 'Why, yes,' I replied. 'I always get a little nervous before I stand up before an audience. I have a profound respect for an audience and the responsibility makes me a bit nervous. Don't you get nervous?'

" No; he said, 'Why should I? Audiences fall for anything. They are a lot of dopes.'

" 'I don't agree with you,' I said. They are your sovereign judges. I have great respect for audiences.' "

When he read about this man's waning popularity Dr. Peale was sure the reason lay in an attitude that antagonized others instead of winning them.

What an object lesson for all of us who want to impart something to other people!

FIFTH

Begin in a Friendly Way

An atheist once challenged William Paley to disprove his

contention that there was no Supreme Being. Very quietly Paley took out his watch, opened the case, and said: "If I were to tell you that those levers and wheels and springs made themselves and fitted themselves together and started running on their own account, wouldn't you question my intelligence? Of course, you would. But look up at the stars. Every one of them has its perfect appointed course and motion—the earth and planets around the sun, and the whole group pitching along at more than a million miles a day. Each star is another sun with its own group of worlds, rushing on through space like our own solar system. Yet there are no collisions, no disturbance, no confusion. All quiet, efficient, and controlled. Is it easier to believe that they just happened or that someone made them so?"

Suppose he had retorted to his antagonist at the outset: "No God? Don't be a silly ass. You don't know what you are talking about." What would have happened? Doubtlessly a verbal joust—a wordy war would have ensued, as futile as it was fiery. The atheist would have risen with an unholy zeal upon him to fight for his opinions with all the fury of a wildcat. Why? Because, as Professor Overstreet has pointed out, they were *his* opinions, and his precious, indispensable self-esteem would have been threatened; his pride would have been at stake.

Since pride is such a fundamentally explosive characteristic of human nature, wouldn't it be the part of wisdom to get a man's pride working for us, instead of against us? How? By showing, as Paley did, that the thing we propose is very similar to something that our opponent already believes. That renders it easier for him to accept than to reject your proposal. That prevents contradictory and opposing ideas from arising in the mind to vitiate what we have said.

Paley showed delicate appreciation of how the human

mind functions. Most men, however, lack this subtle ability to enter the citadel of a man's beliefs arm in arm with the owner. They erroneously imagine that in order to take the citadel, they must storm it, batter it down by a frontal attack. What happens? The moment hostilities commence, the drawbridge is lifted, the great gates are slammed and bolted, the mailed archers draw their long bows—the battle of words and wounds is on. Such frays always end in a draw; neither has convinced the other of anything.

This more sensible method I am advocating is not new It was used long ago by Saint Paul. He employed it in that famous address of his to the Athenians on Mars Hill—employed it with an adroitness and finesse that compels our admiration across nineteen centuries. He was a man of finished education; and, after his conversion to Christianity, his eloquence made him its leading advocate. One day he arrived at Athens—the post-Pericles Athens, an Athens that had passed the summit of its glory and was now on the decline. The Bible says of it at this period: "All the Athenians and strangers which were there spent their time in nothing else but either to tell or to hear some new thing."

No radios, no cables, no news dispatches; those Athenians must have been hard put in those days to scratch up something fresh every afternoon. Then Paul came. Here was something new. They crowded about him, amused, curious, interested. Taking him to the Aeropagus, they said: "May we know what this new doctrine, whereof thou speakest, is? For thou bringest certain strange things to our ears: we would know therefore what these things mean."

In other words, they invited a speech; and, nothing loath, Paul agreed. In fact, that was what he had come for. He probably stood up on a block or stone, and, being a bit nervous, as all good speakers are at the very outset, he may have given his hands a dry wash, and have cleared his throat before he began.

However, he did not altogether approve of the way they had worded their invitation; "New doctrines... strange things." That was poison. He must eradicate those ideas. They were fertile ground for the propagating of contradictory and clashing opinions. He did not wish to present his faith as something strange and alien. He wanted to tie it up to, liken it to, something they already believed. That would smother dissenting suggestions. But how? He thought a moment; hit upon a brilliant plan; he began his immortal address: "Ye men of Athens, I perceive that in all things ye are very superstitious."

Some translations read, "Ye are very religious." I think that is better, more accurate. They worshipped many gods; they were very religious. They were proud of it. He complimented them, pleased them. They began to warm toward him. One of the rules of the art of effective speaking is to support a statement by an illustration. He does just that:

"For, as I passed by, and beheld your devotions, I found an altar with this inscription, TO THE UNKNOWN GOD "

That proves, you see, that they were very religious. They were so afraid of slighting one of the deities that they had put up an altar to the unknown God, a sort of blanket insurance policy to provide against all unconscious slights and unintentional oversights. Paul, by mentioning this specific altar, indicated that he was not dealing in flattery; he showed that his remark was a genuine appreciation born of observation.

Now, here comes the consummate rightness of this opening: "Whom therefore ye ignorantly worship, Him declare I unto you."

"New doctrine...strange things?" Not a bit of it. He was

there merely to explain a few truths about a God they were already worshipping without being conscious of it. Likening the things they did not believe, you see, to something they already passionately accepted—such was his superb technique.

He pronounced his doctrine of salvation and resurrection, quoted a few words from one of their own Greek poets; and he was done. Some of his hearers mocked, but others said, "We will hear thee again on this matter."

Our problem in making a talk to convince or impress others is just this: to plant the idea in their minds and to keep contradicting and opposing ideas from arising. He who is skilled in doing that has power in speaking and influencing others. Here is precisely where the rules in my book *How to Win Friends and Influence People* will be helpful.

Almost every day of your life you are talking to people who differ from you on some subject under discussion. Aren't you constantly trying to win people to your way of thinking, at home, in the office, in social situations of all kinds? Is there room for improvement in your methods? How do you begin? By showing Lincoln's tact and Macmillan's? If so, you are a person of rare diplomacy and extraordinary discretion. It is well to remember Woodrow Wilson's words, "If you come to me and say, 'Let us sit down and take counsel together, and, if we differ from one another, understand why it is that we differ from one another, just what the points at issue are,' we will presently find that we are not so far apart after all, that the points on which we differ are few and the points on which we agree are many, and that if we only have the patience and the candor and the desire to get together, we will get together."

The success of your presentation will be judged not by the knowledge you send but by what the listener receives.

—Lilly Walters

You have it easily in your power to increase the sum total of this world's happiness now. How? By giving a few words of sincere appreciation to someone who is lonely or discouraged. Perhaps you will forget tomorrow the kind words you say today, but the recipient may cherish them over a lifetime.

—Dale Carnegie

Chapter 14

IMPROMPTU TALKS

Not long ago a group of business leaders and government officials met at the dedication of a pharmaceutical corporation's new laboratory. One after another, half a dozen subordinates to the research director arose and told of the fascinating work being done by chemists and biologists. They were developing new vaccines against communicable diseases, new antibiotics to fight viruses, new tranquilizers to ease tension. Their results, first with animals and then with human beings, were dramatic.

"This is marvelous," an official said to the research director. "Your men are really magicians. But why aren't you up there, speaking, too?"

"I can talk to my feet—not to an audience," the research director said gloomily.

A little later, the chairman took him by surprise.

"We haven't heard from our director of research," he said. "He doesn't like to give a formal speech. But I'm going to ask him to say a few words to us."

It was pitiful. The director stood up and managed no

more than a couple of sentences. He apologized for not speaking at length, and that was the gist of his contribution.

There he was, a brilliant man in his field, and he seemed as awkward and confused as a man could be. This was not necessary. He could have learned to speak impromptu on his feet. I have never seen a serious and determined member of our classes who couldn't learn this. At the start, it takes what this research director hadn't given it—a resolute and brave rejection of one's defeatist attitude. Then, perhaps for quite a while, it takes an unwavering will to do the job no matter how hard it may be.

"I get along all right if I've prepared my talk and practiced it," you may say. "But I'm at a loss for words if I'm asked to talk when I don't expect it."

The ability to assemble one's thoughts and to speak on the spur of the moment is even more important, in some ways, than the ability to speak only after lengthy and laborious preparation. The demands of modern business and the current casualness with which modern oral communication is carried on make it imperative to be able to mobilize our thoughts quickly and verbalize fluently. Many of the decisions that affect industry and government today are made, not by one man, but around the conference table. The individual still has his say, but what he has to say has to be forcefully stated in the forum of group opinion. This is where the ability to speak impromptu comes alive and produces results.

FIRST

Practice Impromptu Speaking

Anyone of normal intelligence who possesses a fair portion of self-control can make an acceptable, often a brilliant, impromptu talk—which simply means "talking off the cuff." There are several ways you can improve your ability to express yourself fluently when called upon suddenly to say a few words. One method is to use a device that some famous movie actors used.

Years ago Douglas Fairbanks wrote an article for *American Magazine* in which he described a game of wits he, Charlie Chaplin, and Mary Pickford played almost every night for two years. It was more than a game. It was practice in that most difficult of all speaking arts—thinking on one's feet. As Fairbanks wrote, the "game" went like this:

Each of us would write a subject on a slip of paper. Then we folded the slips and shook them up. One would draw. Immediately he would have to stand and talk for sixty seconds on that subject. We never used the same subject twice. One night I had to talk on "lampshades." Just try it if you think it is easy. I got through somehow.

But the point is all three of us have sharpened up since we began the game. We know a lot more about a variety of miscellaneous subjects. But, far better than that, we are learning to assemble our knowledge and thoughts on any topic at a moment's notice. We are learning how to think on our feet.

Several times during my course the class members are asked to talk impromptu. Long experience has taught me that this kind of practice does two things: (1) it proves to the people in the class that they can think on their feet, and (2) this experience makes them much more secure and confident when they are giving their prepared talks. They realize that, if the worst should happen and they experience a blackout while giving their prepared material, they still can talk intelligently on an impromptu basis until they get back on the track again.

So, at one time or another, the class member hears, "Tonight each of you will be given a different subject on which to talk. You won't know what it is until you stand up to speak. Good luck!"

What happens? An accountant finds he is called on to speak about advertising. An advertising salesman has to talk on kindergartens. A schoolteacher's topic may be banking, and a banker's topic may be school teaching. A clerk may be assigned to talk on production, and a production expert may be asked to discuss transportation.

Do they hang their heads, and give up? Never! They don't pretend to be authorities. They work the subjects around to fit their knowledge of something familiar to them. In their first efforts, they may not give a fine talk. But they *do* get up; they *do* talk. For some it is easy; for some it is hard, but they don't give up; they all find that they can do far better than they'd thought they would. This is thrilling to them. They see that they can develop an ability which they didn't believe they had.

I believe that if they can do this, anybody can do it—with will power and confidence—and that the more often one tries to do it, the easier it will be.

Another method we use to train people to speak on their feet is the linkage technique of impromptu speaking. It is a stimulating feature of one of our class sessions. One class member is told to begin a story in the most fantastic terms he can invent. For instance he might say, "The other day I was piloting my helicopter when I noticed a swarm of flying saucers approaching. I started to descend. But a little man in the nearest saucer started to open fire. I..."

At this point a bell sounds indicating the end of this speaker's time, and the next class member in line must continue the story. By the time everyone in the class has contributed his share, the action may end along the canals of Mars or in the halls of Congress.

This method of developing skill in speaking without

preparation is admirable as a training device. The more such practice a person gets the better he will be qualified to meet the real situations that may arise when he has to speak "for keeps" in his business and social life.

SECOND

Be Mentally Ready to Speak Impromptu

When you are called on to speak without preparation usually you are expected to make some remarks about a subject upon which you can speak with authority. The problem here is to face up to the situation of talking and to decide what exactly you want to cover in the short time at your disposal. One of the best ways to become adept at this is to prepare yourself mentally for these situations. When you are at a meeting keep asking yourself what you would say now if you were called upon. What aspect of your subject would be most appropriate to cover at this time? How would you phrase your approval or rejection of the proposals now being put forth on the floor?

So the first bit of advice I offer is this: condition yourself mentally to speak impromptu on all occasions.

This requires thinking on your part, and thinking is the hardest thing in the world to do. But I am certain that no man ever made a reputation as an impromptu speaker who did not prepare himself by devoting hours of analysis to every public situation in which he was a participant. Just as an airline pilot readies himself to act with cool precision in an emergency by continually posing to himself problems that could arise at any moment, the man who shines as an impromptu speaker prepares himself by making countless talks that are never given. Such talks really are not "impromptu"; they are talks with general preparation.

Because your subject is known, your problem is one of organization to fit the time and the occasion. As an impromptu speaker you will naturally speak for only a short time. Decide what aspect of your topic would fit the situation. Don't apologize because you are unprepared. This is the expected thing. Launch into your topic as soon as possible, if not immediately, and please, I beg you, follow this advice.

THIRD

Get into an Example Immediately

Why? For three reasons: (1) You will free yourself at once of the necessity to think hard about your next sentence, for experiences are easily recounted even in an impromptu situation. (2) You will get into the swing of speaking, and your first-moment jitters will fly away, giving you the opportunity to warm up to your subject matter. (3) You will enlist the attention of your audience at once. As pointed out in Chapter Seven, the incident-example is a sure-fire method of capturing attention immediately.

An audience absorbed in the human interest aspect of your example will give you reassurance when you need it most—during the first few moments of speaking. Communication is a two-way process; the speaker who captures attention is immediately aware of it. As he notes the receptive forces and feels the glow of expectancy, like an electric current, play over the heads of his audience, he is challenged to go on, to do his best, to respond. The rapport thus established between speaker and audience is the key to all successful speaking—without it true communication is impossible. That is why I urge you to begin with an example, especially when you are called on to say a few words.

FOURTH

Speak with Animation and Force

As has been said several times before in this book, if you

speak with energy and forcefulness, your external animation will have a beneficial effect upon your mental processes. Have you ever watched a man in a conversational group who suddenly begins to gesture as he speaks? Soon he is talking fluently, sometimes brilliantly, and he begins to attract a group of eager listeners. The relation of physical activity to the mind is a close one. We use the same words to describe manual and mental operations; for instance, we say "we grasp an idea," or "we clutch at a thought." Once we get the body charged up and animated, as William James pointed out, we very soon will get the mind functioning at a rapid pace. So my advice to you is to throw yourself with abandon into your talk and you will help to insure your success as an impromptu speaker.

FIFTH

Use the Principle of the Here and Now

The time will come when someone will tap you on the shoulder and say "How about a few words?" Or it might come without warning at all. You are relaxed and enjoying the remarks of the master of ceremonies when suddenly you realize he is talking about you. Everybody turns in your direction and before you know it you are introduced as the next speaker.

In this kind of situation your mind is apt to shoot off, like Stephen Leacock's famous but befuddled horseman, who got on his horse "and made off in all directions." Now, if ever, is the time to remain calm. You can get a breather as you address the chairman. Then it is best to stay close to the meeting in the remarks you make. Audiences are interested in themselves and what they are doing. There are three sources therefore from which you can draw ideas for an impromptu speech.

First is the audience itself. Remember this, I pray you,

for easy speaking. Talk about your listeners, who they are and what they are doing, especially what specific good they perform to the community or for humanity. Use a specific example.

The *second* is the occasion. Surely you can dwell on the circumstances that brought the meeting about. Is it an anniversary, a testimonial, an annual meeting, a political or patriotic occasion?

Lastly, if you have been an attentive listener, you might indicate your pleasure in something specific another speaker said before you and amplify that. The most successful impromptu talks are those that are really impromptu. They express things that the speaker feels in his heart about the audience and the occasion. They fit the situation like hand in glove. They are tailor-made for this occasion, and this occasion alone. Therein lies their success: they flower out of the moment and then, like rare-blossoming roses, they fade from the scene. But the pleasure enjoyed by your audience lives on, and sooner than you think you begin to be looked upon as an impromptu speaker.

SIXTH

Don't Talk Impromptu — Give an Impromptu Talk

There is a difference as implied in the statement above. It is not enough just to ramble on and string together a series of disconnected nothings on a flimsy thread of inconsequence. You must keep your ideas logically grouped around a central thought which might well be the point you want to get across. Your examples will cohere to this central idea. And again, if you speak with enthusiasm, you will find that what you say off the cuff has a vitality and punch that your prepared talks do not have.

You can become a competent impromptu speaker if you take to heart some of the suggestions made in this chapter.

You can practice along lines of the classroom techniques explained in the early part of this chapter.

At a meeting you can do a little preliminary planning and you can keep yourself aware of the possibility of being called upon at any moment If you think you may be asked to contribute your comments or suggestions, pay careful attention to the other speakers. Try to be ready to condense your ideas into a few words. When the time comes, say what you have in mind as plainly as you can. Your views have been sought. Give them briefly, and sit down.

Norman Bel-Geddes, the architect and industrial designer, used to say that he couldn't put his thoughts into words unless he was on his feet. Pacing up and down his office, as he talked to associates about complex plans for building or exhibit, he was at his best. He had to learn how to speak when sitting down, and of course he did.

With most of us, it's the other way around; we have to learn to speak standing up, and of course we can. The chief secret lies in making a start—giving one short talk—and then making another start, and another, and another.

We will find that each successive talk comes more easily. Each talk will be better than its predecessors. We will realize in the end speaking impromptu to a group is merely an extension of the same thing we do when we speak impromptu to friends in our living room.

It usually takes me more than three weeks to prepare a good impromptu speech.

—Mark Twain

When dealing with people, remember you are not dealing with creatures of logic, but creatures of emotion.

—Dale Carnegie